GALEN AND THE
SYLLOGISM

GALEN
AND THE SYLLOGISM

An Examination of the Thesis
that Galen Originated the Fourth Figure of the Syllogism
in the Light of New Data from Arabic Sources

including

An Arabic Text Edition and Annotated Translation of
Ibn al-Ṣalāḥ's Treatise
" On the Fourth Figure of the Categorical Syllogism "

by

NICHOLAS RESCHER
Professor of Philosophy in the University of Pittsburgh

UNIVERSITY OF PITTSBURGH PRESS
1966

Library of Congress Catalog Number 66–12132

166
R 31g
59988
Jan. 1968

Printed in England by Stephen Austin & Sons, Ltd., Hertford

Its author cordially dedicates the book to
his colleague and friend

KURT   BAIER

PREFACE

While much remains obscure in our picture of the origination of the fourth syllogistic figure, the received opinion of present-day authorities that Galen had nothing to do with the matter is certainly incorrect. Its plausibility crumbles when one looks at the issue in the light of the relevant materials afforded by Arabic sources. One of the main aims of the present study is to set the record straight and to rehabilitate Galen's claims to a prominent role in launching this logical innovation on its long and checkered career. (A prior preliminary report of some of the findings at issue here was given in a paper entitled " New Light from Arabic Sources on Galen and the Fourth Figure of the Syllogism " published in the *Journal of the History of Philosophy*, vol. 3, 1965, pp. 27–41.)

The present work falls within a series of studies of Arabic logic supported by research grants from the National Science Foundation. Without this assistance my research would have been difficult if not impossible. Nor could it have seen the light of print without the Foundation's contribution to the publication costs. It affords me much pleasure to record my appreciative thanks for this support.

I am grateful to the authorities of the Aya Sofya Museum (and in particular its director, Dr. Sabahattin Batur) both for furnishing me with a microfilm of the Ibn al-Ṣalāḥ manuscript, and for affording me the opportunity to work with the manuscript itself during a visit to Istanbul in September, 1964. Dr. Salih Tuğ of the Islam Institute of the University of Istanbul was so kind as to take me in hand and " show me the ropes " in the magnificent libraries of this great city ; and the hospitality of Dr. Aylā König made my stay there a pleasant and memorable one. My visit, undertaken as a side-excursion during a trip to the Near East on other business, was made possible by a research grant from the Humanities Division of the University of Pittsburgh, which is herewith acknowledged with thanks.

I am grateful to Miss Dorothy Henle for her care in preparing the English typescript for the printer, and for help with proofreading and preparing the Index. Salwa (Mrs. Souren) Teghrarian prepared the Arabic typescript with great care. Finally, I owe special thanks to Professor Michael E. Marmura of the University of Toronto for checking my translation of the Ibn al-Ṣalāḥ text.

N. R.

Pittsburgh
February 1965

CONTENTS

Chapter I

THE ARABIC DATA REGARDING GALEN
AND THE FOURTH FIGURE OF THE SYLLOGISM

1. The Problem of the Origin of the Fourth Syllogistic Figure

Flying in the face of the long-standing tradition—going back in Europe to Renaissance times—which credits Galen of Pergamon with the origination of the fourth figure of the (categorical) syllogism, recent authorities have almost to a man evinced doubt about Galen's claim to this innovation. Heinrich Scholz speaks of " the Galenian syllogistic figure which has been attributed to him, probably wrongly ".[1] J. W. Stakelum concludes his careful discussion of the matter with the categorical assertion that " Galen did not teach the fourth figure ".[2] I. M. Bochenski—following Lukasiewicz (see below)—says that the fourth figure " was only ascribed to Galen by a misunderstanding ".[3] William Kneale (also following Lukasiewicz) writes that " it is easy to see how misunderstanding . . . by some Arabian philosopher . . . could have given rise to the tradition that Galen added a fourth figure to Aristotle's syllogistic theory ".[4] L. M. de Rijk asserts that " it is an established fact that they [the fourth-figure moods] do not come from Galenus ".[5]

The currently accepted account of the matter is that of Jan Lukasiewicz, who in his book on *Aristotle's Syllogistic*[6] presents the known

[1] *Abriss der Geschichte der Logik* (Münster, 1931) ; English tr. by K. F. Leidecker, *Concise History of Logic* (New York, 1961) ; p. 38 of the English version.

[2] " Why ' Galenian ' Figure ? " *The New Scholasticism*, vol. 16 (1942), pp. 289–296.

[3] *Formale Logik* (München-Freiburg, 1956 ; 2d ed., 1962) ; English tr. by Ivo Thomas, *A History of Formal Logic* (Notre Dame, 1961), p. 142 of the English version.

[4] William and Martha Kneale, *The Development of Logic* (Oxford, 1962), p. 184.

[5] *Petrus Abaelardus Dialectica*, ed. L. M. de Rijk (Assen, 1956), p. lxiv.

[6] Oxford, 1951 ; 2d ed., 1957.

reports about Galen and the fourth figure as follows (here listed in the order in which they came to light) :—

(1) Several passages in Averroes' (d. 1198) *Middle Commentary on Prior Analytics* credit Galen with introducing a fourth figure (*ad Anal. Pr.* i : 5, i : 8, and i : 23).[7] These passages—known in Europe through a Renaissance Latin translation of a Hebrew version—provided the basis upon which Jacob Zabarella in his work *De quarta syllogismorum figura*[8] popularized the " Galenian figure " in European logic.

(2) In 1844 Minoides Minas published in the preface to his edition of Galen's *Eisagōgē dialektikē* (Paris, 1844) an anonymous Greek fragment (late, perhaps 6th century) which states that certain " later scholars " transformed the group of syllogisms stressed by Theophrastus and Eudemus as representing indirect moods of the first figure into a new fourth figure, citing Galen as the originator of this doctrine.[9]

(3) About 1858 Carl Prantl found a Greek fragment in a logical work of the Byzantine scholar Ioannes Italus (11th century) which says that Galen taught the existence of a fourth figure, adding sarcastically that he (Galen) thought thus to appear cleverer than the older logical commentators (presumably Theophrastus and Eudemus are intended), but fell far short.[10]

(4) In 1899 Maximilian Wallies published [11] an anonymous Greek scholium (of perhaps the 6th or the 7th century) on Ammonius' commentary on *Prior Analytics* which states that Galen " says in his *Apodictic* that there are four figures, because he looks at the compound syllogisms consisting of four terms [i.e., with three premisses] " rather than the simple (three term, two premiss) syllogisms of Aristotle. (The scholiast goes on to explain at some length how such compound syllogisms can be sorted into four groups.)

It is readily seen that, given these data, the alternative theories before us are :—

(i) Galen did actually invent the traditional fourth figure. Reports (1)–(3) are substantially correct, and the Anonymous Scholiast of (4) was put on the wrong track because Galen said somewhere that compound syllogisms of four terms can be classed into four groups.

---

[7] See Carl Prantl, *Geschichte der Logik im Abendlande*, vol. I (Leipzig, 1855 ; photo-reprinted, Graz, 1955), p. 571.

[8] *Opera* (Leiden, 1587), pp. 41–53 [other editions cited in our References]. Zabarella remarks that *in libris enim Galeni, qui nunc extant, nil de hac figura legimus*, a situation which still obtains today.

[9] Also printed in C. Prantl, *Geschichte der Logik in Abendlande*, vol. I (*op. cit.*), p. 572, n. 100 ; and in Karl Kalbfleisch, " Ueber Galen's Einleitung in die Logik," *23. Supplementband der Jahrbücher für klassische Philologie* (Leipzig, 1897), p. 707. This datum casts doubt upon the suggestion of W. Kneale that the fourth figure originates from a " misunderstanding . . . by some Arabian philosopher," for it suggests that whatever " misunderstanding " there is, was present already in Greek tradition.

[10] Carl Prantl, *Geschichte der Logik im Abendlande*, vol. II (Leipzig, 1885 ; reprinted Graz, 1955), p. 302, n. 112.

[11] M. Wallies (ed.), *Ammonii in Aristotelis Analyticorum Priorum librum I Commentarium* (Berlin, 1899), p. ix.

(ii) Galen did not invent the traditional fourth figure. Only after his time, when the indirect moods of the first figure had—somehow (and this is now an enigma)—become systematized into a separate " figure ", was the fourth figure credited to Galen by a mistake along the lines described by the anonymous scholiast. Thus (4) alone is right, and (1)–(3) are mistaken.

Which of these alternatives are we to choose ? *Prima facie* (ii) seems the less plausible choice because it sets one single report against a group of others involving substantial temporal and geographic spread. But Lukasiewicz unhesitatingly opted for alternative (ii)—albeit without much explanation of why he prefers it to (i)—and, as we have seen, later writers on the subject have, to a man, followed his lead. Misunderstanding, however, is a two-way street, and the fault could surely lie on the side of the Anonymous Scholiast of report (4), instead of that of the rest of the field.

One relevant and apparently significant further consideration is that *the one and only logical treatise of Galen's which we possess in the Greek original*, the very brief logic-manual *Eisagōgē dialektikē*,[12] speaks of the familiar three figures in the usual way, including the standard observation that these are the only figures.[13] But this negative finding can hardly be counted as decisive—as is unhesitatingly done by virtually all contemporary authorities—when once one stops to consider (*inter alia*) that the tract in question is but one minor work of a writer who returned to the subject many times over many years, and further that it is a routine textbook or manual devoted to standard fundamentals, not a treatise devoted to any more far-reaching purpose,[14] in which the presentation of some novel conception of the matters at issue might be undertaken.[15]

The present study will cite evidence that the current rejection of Galen's authorship of the fourth figure is unwarranted. We shall endeavor to show that datum (1), the long-mistrusted report of Averroes, is in fact the crucial consideration and must be given a

---

[12] The most recent studies are : Jürgen Mau, *Galen : Einführung in die Logik*, Berlin (Deutsche Akademie der Wissenschaften zu Berlin), 1960 ; and John S. Kieffer, *Galen's " Institutio Logica,"* Baltimore (Johns Hopkins University Press), 1964. See also the References at the end of this book.

[13] Galen says *tout court* that categorical syllogisms can occur in only the three orthodox figures and that there are no more. He says this has been shown in his treatise *Notes on Demonstration* (§ xii, 1st para.). His way of putting the matter could plausibly be construed to suggest that the issue of the syllogistic figures and their number had been raised as a point of discussion.

[14] Galen's own statement to this effect (at § xi, 2nd para.) should not be overlooked.

[15] There is moreover the certainly significant fact (to which we must return below) that no surviving text by any identifiable logician of antiquity speaks of a fourth syllogistic figure, nor *a fortiori* of a connection between it and Galen.

probative weight far beyond that which any writer on the problem has to date accorded it. It is our thesis that Averroes' report—seemingly late, isolated, and dubious—becomes in fact the most significant and telling item of evidence we possess, when once it is viewed against the background of its context in the Arabic logical tradition.

We do not pretend that the problem of the syllogistic figures is one of fundamental import for logical theory, agreeing entirely with the remark of Lukasiewicz :—

> There are some controversial problems connected with the Aristotelian logic that are of historical interest without having any great logical importance. Among these is the problem of the syllogistic figures.

Despite this fact, the problem has exerted upon modern interpreters of Aristotle's logic something of the fascination of the glare of the cobra for its prey.[16] We enter upon this well-trodden area primarily for three reasons : (1) to present heretofore unknown data from Arabic sources bearing upon the history of the fourth figure, (2) to explore the history of the syllogistic figures in its own right, as an exercise in the " history of ideas " capable of throwing important light upon the evolution of logical tradition both in the orbit of Islam and in Europe, and (3) to analyze perhaps more fully and clearly than has been done elsewhere the logical considerations that are at issue in the debate about the number of syllogistic figures.

2. *Arabic Knowledge of Galen's Logical Writings*

In broaching the topic of the probative weight of Arabic reports linking Galen with the fourth syllogistic figure, the starting-point of our enquiry must be the question of Arabic access to Galen's writings in general,[17] and his logical writings in particular. This question can be answered in a surprisingly easy and decisive way by the survival of the conspectus of his own (and his collaborators') Galen-translations by

[16] The most recent book on Aristotle's logic, Günther Patzig's *Die Aristotelische Syllogistik* (Göttingen, 1959 ; Abhandlungen der Akademie der Wissenschaften in Göttingen, Philologisch-historische Klasse, 3te Folge, Nr. 42), devotes over one-fifth of its space to it. Lukasiewicz himself devotes to it five of the thirty-five sections of his book that deal with the assertoric (non-modal) syllogistic.

[17] A monograph on Galen's influence upon Arabic philosophy is much needed. The brief note by De Lacy O'Leary, " The Influence of Galen on Arabic Philosophy," (*Journal of Indian History*, vol. 2 [1922–23], pp. 233–238) is at best a meager beginning. But see S. Pines' Introduction to his translation of *The Guide of the Perplexed* by Maimonides ([Chicago, 1963], pp. lxxvii–lxxviii), and the remarks on Galen in F. Rosenthal, " The Technique and Approach of Muslim Historical Scholarship," *Analecta Orientalia*, vol. 24 (1947), 74 pp.

the great scholar Ḥunain ibn Isḥāq (809–877),[18] who was uniquely important as a translator into Syriac and Arabic of Greek medical and philosophical texts. Written in parallel to Galen's register of his own writings,[19] this precious document—edited and translated over a generation ago by the eminent German Arabist Gotthelf Bergsträsser[20]—affords a microscopically detailed view of the accessibility in Arabic of Galen's logical works in the scholarly community of Baghdad around 900 A.D. We learn of the avid interest in Galen's every word and the painstaking efforts with which his writings were assembled and studied. Although interest focussed primarily on the medical writings of the great physician, every effort was made to examine his logical works as well, with the result that Arabic scholars of the period possessed a view of the logical teachings of the great Pergamite better than any that we moderns can ever hope to possess.

To give some indication of the extraordinary lengths to which Ḥunain and his younger collaborators went to make Galen's writings available, we shall cite *in extenso* his entry for Galen's *Peri apodeixeōs* (*De demonstratione: fī 'l-burhān*) :—

> He (Galen) wrote this book in fifteen chapters. He pursues in it the aim of examining how one must necessarily proceed in the demonstration of something demonstrable. This was [also] the aim of Aristotle in the fourth of his books of logic (= the *Posterior Analytics*). Up to the present time none of our contemporaries has found a complete Greek MS of *Peri apodeixeōs*, although Jibrīl (ibn Bakhtīshūʿ ?)[21] made great efforts in searching for one. I myself searched for it thoroughly, and in searching for it traveled through Mesopotamia and Syria, Palestine and Egypt. Until I reached Alexandria I found none of it, except for about half of it in Damascus, but in non-consecutive and incomplete parts (chapters). Jibrīl also found some parts of it which were not all identical with the parts I found. Ayyub[22] translated for him the parts he had found. But as for me, I could not decide to translate some of them without bringing their reading to a completion, because of the incomplete and fragmented state in which they were, and the eagerness and yearning of my soul to find this complete book. At last I translated into Syriac what I had found, namely a fragment of the second chapter, the bulk of the third chapter, about

---

[18] For his bio-bibliography see N. Rescher, *The Development of Arabic Logic* (Pittsburgh, 1964), pp. 103–105.

[19] *Galēnou peri tēs taxeōs tōn idiōn bibliōn* in *Claudii Galeni Opera Omnia*, ed. C. G. Kühn, vol. 19 (Leipzig, 1830).

[20] " Ḥunain ibn Isḥāq über die syrischen und arabischen Galen-Uebersetzungen," *Abhandlungen für die Kunde des Morgenlandes*, vol. 17 (1925), no. 2.

[21] For this important scholar, physician to the caliph Hārūn al-Rashīd, see Georg Graf, *Geschichte der christlichen arabischen Literatur*, vol. II (Vatican City, 1947 ; Studi e Testi, no. 133), p. 110.

[22] For Ayyub ibn al-Qāsim al-Raqqī (fl. ca. 820) see N. Rescher, *The Development of Arabic Logic* (*op. cit.*), p. 96.

half of the fourth chapter starting at the beginning, and the ninth chapter except for a part at the beginning, which was lost. As for the remaining chapters [viz., ten to fifteen], I found them all up to the end of the book, except for the fifteenth chapter, for there was a gap at its end. ʿĪsā ibn Yaḥyā [23] translated (into Arabic) what he (Ḥunain) had found, from the second to the eleventh chapter, and Isḥāq ibn Ḥunain [24] translated into Arabic from the twelfth to the fifteenth chapter.[25]

As this extract indicates, Ḥunain and his younger collaborators spared no efforts to see to it that all of Galen's writings, the logical works not excepted, were made available in Arabic. Specifically, of Galen's almost forty logical treatises, the majority were put into Arabic, in part or whole, by this group. It seems reasonable to conclude that interested scholars of the time and place of Ḥunain could not possibly have been under any significant misapprehension concerning the logical teachings of Galen.

Of course it is a long way from Ḥunain to Averroes, and we must now consider the somewhat sinuous road that linked them together.

3. The Role of Galen's Logical Writings in the Arabic Tradition of Logical Studies

Granting that Galen's logical writings were available to the earliest generation of Arabic logicians, the question remains : Did they play any significant role in the subsequent tradition ? The answer is that they played a critically important one. To see how this was so, we must begin with a dogmatically brief outline of the evolution of Arabic logic.[26]

(1) Logical *studies* as such (in contrast with the *translation* and assimilation of Greek logical treatises) began in an Arabic milieu around 875 A.D. with the inauguration of a logical " School of Baghdad " which flourished in that city for well over a century. By far its most prolific and influential product was al-Fārābī (ca. 873–950), who was exceptional in not knowing Syriac and in being a Muslim : all members of the " school " were Syrian Christians.

[23] Regarding this scholar see N. Rescher, *The Development of Arabic Logic (op. cit.)*, pp. 113–114.

[24] This is the—almost equally celebrated—son of Ḥunain ibn Isḥāq, who lived ca. 845–910/911. For his bio-bibliography see N. Rescher, *The Development of Arabic Logic (op. cit.)*, pp. 111–113,

[25] G. Bergsträsser, *op. cit.*, pp. 47–48 of the Arabic text corresponding to pp. 38–39 of the German translation. The final sentence of the passage is an addendum inserted by a student of Ḥunain's.

[26] This brief sketch is based on the detailed account given in N. Rescher, *The Development of Arabic Logic (op. cit.)*.

(2) A sharply critical reaction against this school was launched by Avicenna (980–1037) and was carried on by his immediate followers. Avicenna advanced his (partially anti-Aristotelian) ideas under the rubric of a rival " Logic of the Easterners ", and attacked the School of Baghdad with both argument and invective—though he tended to make an exception of al-Fārābī in logic and certain members of the school in medicine.

(3) The influence of Avicenna was contested by a small group of " Western " logicians (as we may call them). This rival school was launched by Abū 'l-Barakāt ibn Malkā (ca. 1075–ca. 1170), and its position was consolidated by his principal student Fakhr al-Dīn al-Rāzī (1149–1209). The school flourished from around 1150 to the time of Ibn Kammūnah (ca. 1125–1284).

(4) The logical tradition of the School of Baghdad and especially of al-Fārābī took early root in Spain where it was revivified by Ibn Bājjah (1090–1138) and reached its apex in the work of Averroes (1126–1198). To a man, the Spanish Muslim logicians followed the more orthodox Aristotelianism of al-Fārābī and opposed Avicenna.

(5) The tradition of Avicenna was supported by a group of " Eastern " logicians (as we may call them). This flourishing movement in defense of Avicenna against the Westerners founds its mainstay in the famous scholar and scientist Naṣīr al-Dīn al-Ṭūsī (1201–1274). It was the dominant force in logical studies in Eastern Islam until somewhat after 1300.

(6) The final phase of Arabic logic was inaugurated by the effort of al-Tustarī (ca. 1270–ca. 1330) and his disciple al-Taḥtānī (ca. 1290–1365) to effect an arbitration between the Eastern and Western schools (however with definitely Eastern learnings). The resulting fusion left later Arabic logicians free to draw on both sectors of the tradition, and to make use of the handbooks of both schools for the study and teaching of logic.

The role of Galen in this sequence of developments was a central and crucially important one : indeed to a considerable extent it constitutes the "bone of contention". Galen's departures from Aristotle were known to and discussed by Arabic scholars from the very inception of Arabic knowledge of Greek science. And those few who—like Avicenna—wished to shake off the shackles of Aristotle's unilaterial authority in philosophy looked to the writings of Galen for support. As regards Galen's philosophical and, in particular, his logical works the situation can be summed up as follows :

(1) The School of Baghdad were fully aware of Galen's departures from Aristotle and, in effect, carried forward the more rigid Aristotelianism of Alexander of Aphrodisias by espousing his critique of Galen. Al-Fārābī's critical discussions of Galen's logical views were especially hostile. (For example, in his *Great Commentary on " De Interpretatione "* he treated at some length and explicitly rejects Galen's criticism of Aristotle that it is pointless to deal with syllogisms with contingent premisses, since they have no application in the sciences.[27] And we possess a report of Maimonides that

[27] W. Kutsch, S.J. and S. Marrow, S.J. (ed's), *Alfarabi's Commentary on Aristotle's " Peri Hermēneias "* (Beirut, 1960), p. 193.

in his *Great Commentary on "Analytica Priora"* al-Fārābī makes extensive criticisms of Galen's views on modal propositions and modal syllogisms.[28])

(2) Avicenna, who made free to depart from Aristotle, tended to do so not wholly on his own, but under the influence of ancient authorities rival to Aristotle, particularly Galen and the Stoics. The same spirit which led him to make departures from Galen in medicine led Avicenna occasionally to draw upon him as an ally against Aristotle in philosophy.[29]

(3) The Spanish Muslim philosophers allied themselves with the more orthodox Aristotelianism of al-Fārābī, and were hostile to the innovations represented by Avicenna's departures from the master.[30]   They were of course also opposed to Galen in philosophy, as we know from the critique of Averroes. (It is no accident that several of Alexander of Aphrodisias' series of " Refutations of Galen " on various philosophical points have survived only in Arabic translations in a Spanish library.[31])

(4) The Westerners—i.e., the later opponents of Avicenna—tended to hew to more generally orthodox Aristotelian conceptions, taking a dim view of Galen's critique of Aristotle.

(5) The Easterners—i.e., Avicenna's later adherents—tended to go beyond their master in disputing traditionally Aristotelian positions ; thus views that penetrated into Arabic logic from the Stoics or Galen were sometimes preserved (to be sure in a fossilized form) in the logic-manuals of this school.

As this brief survey suggests, Galen's departures from Aristotle came to play a highly significant—indeed pivotal—part in the evolution of logical studies in Islam.

*   *   *

Turning now from a synoptic view of the role of Galen's influence within the Arabic logical tradition, it is necessary to give brief consideration to the question of Averroes' source of information regarding Galen's views on logic. The answer is straightforward. The predominant influence upon the logical tradition of Muslim Spain was—from start to finish—Abū Naṣr al-Fārābī. The direct impact of his extensive writings on the subject was felt by all the logicians of Muslim Spain, and is clearly traceable in both the well-known writers (Ibn Bājjah, Maimonides, Averroes) and in the obscure ones (e.g., the several authors of the short logic-tracts circulated during the

[28] M. Steinschneider, *Al-Fārābī* (St. Pétersbourg, 1869 ; Mémoires de l'Académie Impériale des Sciences de St. Pétersbourg, series 7, vol. 13, no. 4), pp. 31 ff. (Compare also some of the other discussions listed on p. 259, index, s.v. *Galenus*.)

[29] To say this is not to say that Avicenna acknowledged Galen's influence (say in logic) and overtly spoke well of him as a logician. He did not. (See I. Madkour, *L'Organon d'Aristote dans le monde arabe* [Paris, 1934], p. 207.) Nor did he accept Galen's lead at all points ; e.g., he rejects his views on modal syllogisms. (*Ibid.*, pp. 211–212.)

[30] Avenzoar went so far as to describe the *Qānūn* of Avicenna as " waste paper." D. Campbell, *Arabian Medicine*, vol. 1 (London, 1926), p. 79.

[31] See H. Derenbourg's catalogue of the Escurial library.

8

Renaissance with the Latin translation of the Aristotelian commentaries of Averroes under the rubric *Quaesita ac epistolae in libros logicae Aristotelis*). Averroes cites al-Fārābī's own views on controverted logical matters innumerable times.[32] It is as certain as circumstantial evidence can make it that Averroes' information about Galen and the fourth figure derives directly from al-Fārābī's (lost) [33] great commentary on *Prior Analytics*—and, as was indicated above, it is virtually incredible that al-Fārābī could have been mistaken about this matter. Thus wholly apart from the question of further Arabic data on the issue, Averroes' report is by itself, I submit, an item of evidence to which great probative weight must be assigned.

4. Attitudes Towards the Fourth Figure in Arabic Logical Texts

Many Arabic logical treatises and manuals, and in particular most of those produced under the influence of the Western school, pass over the fourth figure in complete silence.[34] We shall now survey, in chronological sequence, all of those Arabic discussions of the fourth figure—over and above that of Averroes—which have come to our attention.[35]

(1) AVICENNA (980–1037). In his *Kitāb al-ishārāt wā-'l-tanbīhāt* [36] Avicenna discusses not " the fourth figure " but " the inverse of the first ". He does not mention Galen. He does not call this a " figure " (*shakl*) but a " syllogistic construction " (*ibānah qiyāsiyyah*). He calls this reasoning " unnatural " and " rejected ". In short, although he does not ignore the

---

[32] Steinschneider, *Al Fārābī* (*op. cit.*).

[33] There is yet hope of recovering it. In their edition of *Alfarabi's [Great] Commentary on Aristotle's " Peri Hermēneias "* (Beirut, 1960) Fathers W. Kutsch and S. Marrow (S.J.) speak of " other parts of the commentary on the Organon which, we suspect, exist in Teheran " (p. x). Barring the recovery of al-Fārābī's commentary, there exists in the Escorial an elaborate (unpublished) set of glosses upon it, viz. those of Ibn Bājjah (Avempace). (Casiri, codex 609 ; Derenbourg, codex 612.) See also D. M. Dunlop, " Remarks on the Life and Work of Ibn Bājjah [Avempace]," *Proceedings of the 22nd International Congress of Orientalists* [Istanbul, 1951], vol. II (ed. Z. Velidi Togan ; Leiden, 1957), pp. 188-196. These glosses could well prove adequate to our present purpose.

[34] A " great commentary " on *Prior Analytics* would, of course, be an exception, since it would be expected to deal with controverted points. But none has survived, so far as we now know. This silence, incidentally, mirrors that of the Greek commentators—even in their " great commentaries "—and of the Syrian logicians of the 5th and 6th centuries on whom the first generation of Arabic logicians largely relied. (See H. F. Janssens [ed.], *L'Entretien de la Sagesse de Bar Hebraeus* [Paris and Liège, 1937], p. 198.)

[35] Detailed information regarding the various logicians involved here can be found in N. Rescher, *The Development of Arabic Logic* (*op. cit.*).

[36] Ed. J. Forget, *Ibn Sīnā : Le Livre des Théorèmes et des Avertissements* (Leyden, 1892). The relevant passage occurs on pp. 67-68.

fourth figure, he downgrades it.[37] His discussion of the matter in the (just published, but at this writing unavailable) section on *Analytics* (*al-qiyās*) of the *Shifā'* would be a most important datum.[38] Distinguishing the figures in terms of the placement in the premisses (as subject or predicate) of the subject and predicate of the conclusion, Avicenna here arrives at the four theoretically possible figures in the usual way. *He explicitly attributes this procedure to Galen*, but dismisses the fourth figure as unnatural, and treats it in a cursory way, much as in the *Kitāb al-ishārāt*.

(2) ABŪ 'L-BARAKĀT IBN MALKĀ (ca. 1075–ca. 1170). In his *Kitāb al-muʿtabar fi 'l-ḥikmah* [39] this Western scholar describes and discusses the fourth figure. He says that it was not discussed by Aristotle but was introduced " by some later scholars " (*baʿd al-muta'akhirīn*) as a completion of Aristotle's. (There is no mention of Galen.) He regards it as a mere variant of the first figure and does not accord it the exhaustive treatment he gives to the three Aristotelian figures. (A complete translation of this discussion is given in Section 7 below.)

(3) IBN AL-ṢALĀḤ (ca. 1090–1153). To be dealt with below.

(4) ʿABD AL-LAṬĪF (1162–1231). This Western scholar is reported by Arabic bio-bibliographers to have written a tract entitled " Discourse on the falsity of the fourth figure " (*Maqālah fi tazyif al-shakl al-rābiʿ*).[40] It has not survived.

(5) IBN AL-ʿASSĀL (ca. 1190–ca. 1250). In his *Maqālah fi 'l-manṭiq* [41] this author explicitly recognizes and admits the fourth figure, although he says it is " extremely unnatural ".

(6) AL-ABHARĪ (ca. 1200–1265). In his *Īsāghūjī fi 'l-manṭiq*,[42] this Eastern logician lists the fourth figure along with the rest, treating it uniformly with them, without derogatory comment.

(7) NĪAṢR AL-DĪN AL-ṬŪSĪ (1201–1274). This Eastern scholar recognizes the fourth figure,[43] although he treats it in a subordinate way and condemns it as " unnatural ", exactly in the manner of Avicenna.

(8) AL-QAZWĪNĪ AL-KĀTIBĪ (ca. 1220–1292 ?). Pupil of (5). This Eastern scholar in his *Risālah al-shamsiyyah* [44] treats the fourth figure uniformly with the others, like al-Abharī but in much more detail. After

[37] On Avicenna's treatment of the syllogistic figures see I. Madkour, *L'Organon d'Aristote dans le monde arabe* (Paris, 1934), pp. 206-213 and 246-248.

[38] This discussion is summarized briefly in I. Madkour, *ibid.*, pp. 206-207.

[39] Ed. by S. Yaltkaya, Hyderabad, 3 vols., 1358 A.H. (= 1939).

[40] Ibn abī Uṣaibiʿah, *Uyūn*, ed. Müller, vol. II, pp. 212-213.

[41] Ed. Ḥabīb Iddih (= Paul Eddé). *Al-Mashriq* (Arabic language journal published in Beirut), vol. 7 (1904), pp. 811–819 and 1072–1978 (the relevant passage occurs on pp. 1076-7). Republished in L. Cheikho, *Traités inédits d'anciens philosophes arabes* (Beirut, 1911), pp. 133–147.

[42] English translation by Edwin E. Calverly, " Al-Abharī's *Īsāghūjī fi 'l-Manṭiq*, " *The Macdonald Presentation Volume* (Princeton, 1922), pp. 75–85 (the relevant discussion is on pp. 82–83).

[43] See Max Horten, *Die philosophischen Ansichten von Razi und Tusi* (Bonn, 1910), pp. 7, 161.

[44] Arabic text edition and English translation by Aloys Sprenger in *A Dictionary of the Technical Terms Used in the Sciences of the Musulmans*, Part II (Calcutta, 1862), see pp. 20–22 of the Arabic text and pp. 26–30 of the English translation.

listing eight moods as valid for this figure (AAI, IAI, AEE, EAO, EIO, and, oddly enough, AOO, OAO, IEO) he concludes with the remark that " the ancients " (al-mutaqaddimūn) regarded only the first five of these as valid.[45]

(9) BAR HEBRAEUS (1226–1286). Drawing largely on Avicenna, this important Syro-Arabic philosopher-theologian distinguishes the four figures in his *Discourse on Wisdom*.[46] He discusses the fourth figure and treats it uniformly with the other three.[47]

(10) ISAAC ALBALAG (ca. 1250–1310). This Judeo-Arabic philosopher and translator of the *Maqāsid* of al-Ghazzālī wrote a logic-tract of which but a portion is available.[48] He insists on the need for four figures, gives the validity rules of the fourth, and illustrates its valid moods. So far as one can tell from the accessible fragments, Albalag treats the fourth figure in detail and without derogatory comment.

(11) AL-AKHDARĪ (ca. 1514–1546). In *Al-Sullam al-murauniq fī 'l-mantiq*— a highly popular versification of al-Abharī's *Kitāb al-isāghūjī*— this author accords the fourth figure unhesitating acceptance, apart from the remark that the four figures are enumerated " in order of perfection ".[49]

We thus see clear traces of an evolution in the acceptance of the fourth figure in Arabic logic. The earlier logicians take little or no note of the fourth figure, and when they do so at all, they (Avicenna and some of his earliest disciples as well as logicians under the influence of the School of Baghdad) all regard it as " unnatural ". However, later writers in the Eastern tradition are unanimous in an unhesitating

[45] Compare the details regarding the three extra moods given in al-Bajūrī's commentary on al-Akhdarī's *Al-Sullam* (as cited in footnote 49 below), and cf. also the discussion in I. Madkour, *L'Organon d'Aristote dans le monde arabe* (*op. cit.*), pp. 246–247. (Madkour seems unaware that the syllogisms in question are invalid.)

[46] *L'Entretien de la Sagesse de Bar Hebraeus*, ed. H. F. Janssens (Liège and Paris, 1937 ; Bibliothèque de la Faculté de Philosophie et Lettres de l'Université de Liège, fasc. 57), p. 193.

[47] *Ibid.*, pp. 194, 203. See also the translator's discussion on pp. 198–200, noting especially the passage :

Bar Hebraeus attribue [in several of his works] à la quatrième figure du syllogisme la même importance qu'aux autres figures et démontre la validité des modes qu'elle comporte. Il contredit donc, dans ces ouvrages, l'opinion qu'il a émise dans le *Livre des Pupilles* (14a 1 ss.), où il a dit : ' Si le terme moyen est attribut par rapport au mineur et sujet pour rapport au majeur, c'est ce qu'on appelle la première figure ; si c'est l'inverse, c'est qu'on appelle la quatrième figure. Mais celle-ci ne mérite pas d'être mentionée, parce qu'elle n'existe pas vraiment '.

[48] Quoted in I. M. Bochenski, *Formal Logic* (*op. cit.*), pp. 217–218.

[49] French translation by J. D. Luciani, *Le Soullam : Traité de logique* (Algers, 1921), pp. 53–6. (This work also gives the glosses of the editor [Ibrāhīm al-Bajūrī ; d. 1861] of an older edition [Cairo, Imprimerie Orientale, 1314–1315 A.H. (= 1896–97)] who says that al-Abharī's view of the fourth figure is that of " the ancients," but that one widely followed later author accepted eight moods as valid in this figure. The author in question is doubtless al-Qazwīnī al-Kātibī, from whom this information is almost certainly taken.) The view that the figures (i.e., the three orthodox figures) are enumerated in order of perfection goes back at least to Galen's contemporary Appuleius. See C. Prantl, *Geschichte der Logik im Abendlande*, vol. I (*op. cit.*), p. 585.

acceptance of the fourth figure, recognizing it as more or less equal with the others.

In his important study of Avicenna's logic, Ibrahim Madkour cites [50] the fourth syllogistic figure as one of the very few departures which later Arabic logicians made from Avicenna's own codification of Aristotelian logic. However, this approach fails to take note of Avicenna's own positive role in the course of developments. [51] Avicenna's own standard way of defining the figures (with respect to the placement of the middle term as subject or predicate in the minor and major premisses) is conducive to the introduction of a fourth figure ; [52] indeed it renders its *existence* inevitable and leaves only its *naturalness* open to dispute. And it is clear that Avicenna's approach to the matter provided the impetus for that acceptance of a fourth figure which developed primarily in his own tradition (and was most sharply contested by its opponents).

5. *New Data from the Treatise of Ibn al-Ṣalāḥ*

While there is, as we have seen, little difficulty in finding Arabic discussions of the fourth figure, those which explicitly connect it with Galen are harder to come by. Here I am able to report but one new datum, albeit a very important one : the treatise " On the Fourth Figure of the Categorical Syllogism Attributed to Galen" by the mathematician-physician Ibn al-Ṣalāḥ (ca. 1090–1153). This work will occupy our attention at length in Chapters II–IV below. Here we shall only summarize the new data it gives for the history of the fourth figure of the syllogism.

Ibn al-Ṣalāḥ prefixes his discussion of the logic of the fourth figure by a short bibliographical notice which—despite its brevity—is of the greatest value, because it informs us about the contents of several otherwise lost works. These new data are as follows :—

(1) Galen's (now lost) treatises " On Demonstration " ($Περὶ τῆς ἀποδείξεως$) and " On the Number of Syllogisms " ($Περὶ τοῦ τῶν συλλογισμῶν ἀριθμοῦ$) both take the same line on the question of the number of syllogistic figures (*schēmata*)—viz., that there are only the three traditional ones.

[50] *L'Organon d'Aristote dans le monde arabe* (*op. cit.*), p. 246.
[51] To say nothing of the fact that acceptance of the fourth figure in Arabic logic (albeit on a very limited scale) antedates Avicenna (see below).
[52] This differs from al-Fārābī's definition for which see N. Rescher (tr.), *Al-Fārābī's Short Commentary on Aristotle's " Prior Analytics "* (Pittsburgh, 1963), p. 62. On al-Fārābī's characterization, unlike Avicenna's, only three figures are possible.

(2) An unnamed Syrian scholar contemporary with al-Kindī (d. ca. 870) told him that he had, in Syriac translation, a treatise of Galen's in which the fourth figure was discussed.

(3) Al-Fārābī (d. 950) discussed and rejected the fourth figure (presumably in his *Great Commentary on " Prior Analytics "*). His follower Abū 'l-Faraj ibn al-Ṭayyib (d. 1043) did likewise in his *Commentary on " Prior Analytics "*.

(4) Ibn al-Ṣalāḥ himself had in hand an Arabic version of a treatise by an obscure scholar, named Dinḥā the Priest (*Dinḥā al-qass*), a Syrian Christian who flourished around 800. His work dealt *knowledgeably* and *sympathetically* with the topic of " The Fourth Figure of Galen " (see below).

This new datum—which antedates Averroes' report by some forty years and, like that of Avicenna, emanates from an entirely different part of the Islamic world—thus confirms our suspicions. It reinforces, if any reinforcement is needed, the view that the ascription by Arabic logicians of the fourth figure to Galen derives perhaps immediately from Avicenna, but ultimately from al-Fārābī's *Great Commentary on " Prior Analytics "*. And it shows that Arabic scholars had definite documentary evidence linking the fourth figure with Galen.

6. On the Logic of the Fourth Figure and on Syllogistic Terminology

It is necessary to make some brief preparatory observations about the question—for the moment to be considered essentially apart from any historical considerations—of whether there is or is not a fourth figure of the syllogism.[53] In the manner so frequently encountered in discussions of long-disputed questions, the answer is neither *yes* nor *no* but *yes-and-no*, depending upon how a " syllogism " is conceived of. There are two major alternatives :—

(1) We may take a syllogism to be *a pair of undifferentiated premisses* only, considered in the context of the " syllogistic question " of what conclusion follows from them (the conclusion thus being unspecified). (This essentially is the primordial " Aristotelian " construction of the matter.[54]) If *any* syllogistic conclusion whatsoever is to follow, the premisses must share a common mediating term. (There being no indicated conclusion, a question cannot arise as to which of the extreme terms is the predicate of the conclusion and which is its subject : thus there is no discrimination

---

[53] We deal with the matter here in a preliminary way, presenting only what is needed for the historical considerations of the two following sections. The question is taken up again, and in more detail, in Chapter II.

[54] It is also the view of the schoolmen : " It may be observed, that the earliest scholastic Logicians do not consider Mood as composed of three propositions, but of the two premisses only. Thus Petrus Hispanus defines ' ordinatio *duarum* propositionum in debita qualitate et quantitate ' ; so Aquinas in *Opusc.* lxviii, de Syll., ch. 4." H. L. Mansel (ed.), *H. Aldrich : Artis logicae rudimenta* (Oxford, 1852), p. 72, notes.

at the outset between a " major " and a " minor " premiss.[55]   Now with respect to the middle term there are exactly three possibilities : (1) it is the predicate of one premiss and the subject of the other, or (2) it is the predicate of both premisses, or (3) it is the subject of both premisses. From the standpoint of this—to my mind the orthodox Aristotelian—construction of a syllogism, there is no possibility of anything more or less than three figures. (What we regard as the " fourth figure " is simply part of the first.)

(2) We may take a syllogism to be *a pair of premisses combined with a given conclusion*. (This essentially is—to anticipate and to oversimplify somewhat—the strictly Galenian construction of the matter.)   Again, the premisses must be linked by one common term ; and moreover the premisses become distinguished because the (given) subject of the conclusion must be present in one premiss (the " minor ") and the predicate of the conclusion must be present in the other premiss (the " major "). Thus there are now four possibilities as regards the placement of the middle term : (1) it is the predicate of the minor and the subject of the major, (2) it is the predicate of both premisses, (3) it is the subject of both premisses, and (4) it is the predicate of the major and the subject of the minor.[56]   (Specification of the given conclusion makes for a distinction between the premisses and splits the *old* " first figure " into two.[57])   From the standpoint of this " Galenian " construction of a syllogism,[58] one is led to four rather than to three figures.

The disputed question of the correct number of syllogistic figures may thus be seen to turn on the very conception of a syllogism. Is a syllogism to be viewed as what Alexander of Aphrodisias calls a *syzygia*, namely as a *pair* of categorical propositions so linked by one common term as to be capable of serving together as the premisses (only) of a " syllogism " in the modern sense ? Or, is a syllogism to be viewed as what Alexander calls a *symplokē*, that is, as a *trio* of categorical propositions so linked in the overlap of their terms as to be capable of serving together as the premisses *and the conclusion* of a " syllogism " in the modern sense.[59] The

[55] That is, no *formal* discrimination (though there could indeed be a *material* one, drawn on the basis of the inclusiveness [extension] of the terms involved).

[56] The distinction between the two modes of " syllogism " is crucially reflected in how the major and minor terms are to be conceived of—viz. they can be discriminated in terms of their *placement in the conclusion* in this case, but must be distinguished on some other basis (presumably somehow in terms of their relative extension) in the former.

[57] Or the same effect could be achieved by looking on the two premisses as an *ordered* pair, the first of which is to contain the subject of the conclusion.

[58] Avicenna tells us in so many words that Galen arrived at a fourth figure from this angle of approach.   See I. Madkour, *L'Organon d'Aristote dans le monde arabe* (Paris, 1934), p. 206.   Moreover, in § vii of the *Eisagōgē dialektikē* Galen explicitly labels conception (1) as that of " the ancient philosophers " (*hoi palaioi philosophoi*). This would suggest that there are " moderns " (perhaps Stoics ?) who take a different view.

[59] A great deal of confusion resulted in ancient and medieval logical discussions because their authors were faithful to the Master when launching their discussion of

question is not simply one of three *versus* four figures ; it depends on one's conception of a " syllogism " and correspondingly of a " figure ". The (actual or implicit) presence or absence of the conclusion in a " syllogism " is the crucial factor for the question of the number of syllogistic figures.

7. *The Analysis of Abū 'l-Barakāt ibn Malkā*

What follows is a translation from the original Arabic of the section on the fourth figure of the syllogism from the book on logic of the tripartite philosophical *summa* (logic, physics, metaphysics), " The Contemplation of Wisdom " (*Kitāb al-muʿtabar fī 'l-ḥikmah*), of Abū 'l-Barakāt ibn Malkā (ca. 1075–ca. 1170).[60] This report throws much light upon the history of the fourth figure.

*   *   *

(Start of Quotation)

[125 : 7] If the required proposition [i.e., the conclusion] and its two terms are not considered, then no classification [literally : *distinction*] is needed apart from /8/ the three aforementioned figures,[61] since the middle term will [either] be predicated of the two [other] terms, or be subject /9/ for the two terms, or be predicated of one term and be subject for the other, if the two [other] terms are not specified as the subject of the required proposition /10/ and its predicate. For this reason Aristotle constructed three figures and did not mention the fourth. The minor /11/ and the major premisses are only to be distinguished in the first figure by [considering] which [of the premisses] contains the middle term as predicate and as subject : /12/ the one which contains it [the middle term] as predicate is the minor, and the one which contains it as subject is the major. But in /13/ the second and third figures the minor one of the two premisses is not distinguished from the major one of the two by comparing the middle term, /14/ because it [the middle term] is the subject or the predicate in

---

syllogism and figure from the " Aristotelian " way of viewing the matter, but then after a time slipped over in their treatment to what I call the " Galenian " construction of syllogism and figure.

[60] Ed. S. Yaltkaya, 3 vols., Hyberabad, 1358 A.H. (= 1939) ; the passage here presented occurs on pp. 125–6 of vol. I. For Ibn Malkā see N. Rescher, *The Development of Arabic Logic* (*op. cit.*), pp. 169–170.

[61] That is, the three standard Aristotelian figures.

both together. It is distinguished by [considering] the subject and the predicate of the required proposition. /15/ The relationship [of the premisses] to a specified required proposition and its two terms necessitated a fourth figure, for the specified required proposition leads through conversion to its predicate /16/ being subject and its subject being predicate.

For example let that which is required of us be whether *Every man is a creature-that-laughs* or not, as we discussed above. /17/ Then we form a " connection " [of premisses] as follows, *Every articulate creature is a man* and *Every creature-that-laughs is articulate* from which it follows that *Every* /18/ *creature-that-laughs is a man,* which is the converse of the required proposition, since we have put the major term in place of the minor in the " connection " [of premisses] /19/ and the minor in place of the major. Thus if we interchange the two premisses in the formulation of the statement [of the argument], it returns to the form /20/ of the first figure itself. But the interchange of the statement is what is put first and what follows does not alter anything respecting its truth. /21/ Thus it yields its conclusion in a self-evident way. But it [the conclusion] is the converse of the specified required proposition. And if we convert the conclusion /22/ it will be particular—as was recognized in the [discussion of] conversions—so that it renders true [the conclusion], " Some man is a creature-that-laughs ". If [however] /23/ we look at the " connection " [only] without the specified required proposition, we shall not have a form and figure different from /24/ the first figure aside from the preceding and the succeeding of a statement [or : *expression*]. There is no change, therefore, in the truth [of the conclusion] when there is [such] interchange.[62]

[126 : 1] Discussion about this fourth figure was added as supplement to Aristotle by some later scholars, /2/ by taking into account [also]

---

[62] The analysis of this example is as follows. We begin with the valid (AAA-1) syllogism

All A is M
All L is A
All L is M

Since the conclusion entails (through conversion by limitation) that " Some M is L ' we obtain by interchange of premisses the valid (AAI-4) syllogism

All L is A
All A is M
Some M is L

As long as we consider only the premisses, both these syllogisms answer indifferently to Aristotle's " first figure." However, by taking the conclusion into account a difference in their mode of construction is brought out that warrants their assignment to different " figures "—albeit now in somewhat modified sense.

the specified required proposition. In achievement he [Aristotle] is the first and [also] in honor for his achievement. The figures [of the syllogism], /3/ according to him, are the three aforementioned ones [or : *are the three that he mentioned*] and no more.

(End of Quotation)

*   *   *

This way of looking at the question of three *versus* four syllogistic figures is by no means idiosyncratic to Ibn Malkā, but is also encountered in other Arabic logical texts.[63] It is thus clear that some Arabic logicians dealt with the question of the syllogistic figures in just *exactly* the way that we would expect on the basis of the distinction between an Aristotelian two-premisses-cum-question and a Galenian two-premisses-cum-conclusion conception of the syllogism (as sketched in Section 6 above).[64]

8. Terminological Clues that Galen Taught Four Figures

We shall now present some admittedly indirect and circumstantial evidence for the following :

CONJECTURE

Galen distinguished between (1) the three " figures " (sing., *schēma* in Greek and *shakl* in Arabic) of the premisses-only " syllogism " of Aristotle = the syllogistic *syzygia* (*qarīnah* in Arabic) of Alexander of Aphrodisias, and (2) the four " figures " (sing., *systasis* in Greek = *banā'* in Arabic) of the full premisses-cum-conclusion " syllogism " = the syllogistic *symplokē* (*jāmi'ah* in Arabic) of Alexander for which he (Galen) seems to have used the word *technē* (*ṣan'ah* in Arabic).

If this conjecture is correct, Galen did indeed follow the Master in teaching only three standard Aristotelian syllogistic *schēmata*. However, he *also* taught a fourth " figure "—in a rather unemphatic way—in

---

[63] See, for example, " Ibn al-'Assāl : *Maqālah fī 'l-manṭiq*," ed. Ḥabīb Iddih (= Paul Eddé), *Al-Mashriq* (Arabic journal published in Beirut), vol. 7 (1904), pp. 811–819 and 1072–1078 (the relevant passage occurs on pp. 1076–1077. (This was republished in L. Cheikho, *Traités inédits d'anciens philosophes arabes* [Beyrouth, 1911], pp. 133–147.)

[64] Reverberations of this question that occupied the Arabs regarding the place of the conclusion in a " syllogism " are still to be found in Zabarella : *In primis summopere notidum est id, quod dicitur ab Averroe ... necnon ab Alexandro [Aphrodisiensis] ... & ab ipsis quoq : Galeni defensoribus conceditur, ac ponitur, quod syllogismus consideratus ab Aristot. in libris Prioribus Analyticis est, qui constituitur super determinato quaesito, id est super certa aliqua, & statuta conclusione, quae proponitur per syllogismum colligenda. (Liber de quarta syllogismorum figura, caput II ; Opera logica [Basel, 1594], col. 102.)*

17

his discussion of the modes of " construction " (*systasis*) of the syllogistic *technai*, based upon an entirely changed perspective as to what is involved in " syllogism ". This view that Galen largely followed the usual path, and did not set up the question of the syllogistic figures as a significant problematic issue, would account for the fact that no known ancient logical text until after the time of Boethius spoke of a " Galenian figure " or dealt with its syllogisms along lines different from those of Theophrastus and Eudemus.

The following considerations constitute the evidence upon which our conjecture rests :

(1) In ninth-century Arabic translations of Greek logical texts, Greek *technē* standardly becomes Arabic *ṣan'ah*.

(2) In ninth-century Arabic logic texts—but only rarely thereafter—the terms *ṣan'ah* and *banā'* occur on occasion in place of the standard Arabic words for syllogism (*qiyās*) and for " figure " (Arabic *shakl* = Greek *schēma* [65]). Evidence for this assertion is given in the Appendix to this section.

(3) Galen's list of his own works contains several titles of treatises dealing with the characteristics of syllogistic *technai* or with their *systasis*.[66]

(4) Avicenna in one place refers to the indirect (or " inverse "—i.e., those arising by conversion of the conclusion) moods of the first figure as constituting a syllogistic *banā'*.[67]

The equations

$$\text{Arabic } \textit{ṣan'ah} = \text{Greek } \textit{technē}$$
$$\text{Arabic } \textit{banā'} = \text{Greek } \textit{systasis}$$

provide, we submit, a link between Galen and the fourth figure, because we know, on the one hand, that Galen wrote logical treatises on the " construction " (*systasis*) and characteristics of syllogistic *technai* and, on the other hand, that the Arabic words *banā'* and *ṣan'ah* are sometimes used in a corresponding way in connection with syllogistic figures in early Arabic logical texts.[68]

This admittedly circumstantial finding has the significant consequence that, if it is correct, then in examining the evidence for Galen's invention of a fourth figure we must be prepared to discount any statements of his to the effect that there are but three *schēmata* of the

---

[65] On *shakl* see S. M. Afnan, *Philosophical Terminology in Arabic and Persian* (Leiden, 1964), pp. 107–108.

[66] *Opera Omnia*, ed. C. G. Kühn, vol. xix (Leipzig, 1830), pp. 44–45.

[67] Literally he refers to their *ibānah qiyāsiyyah* (*Kitāb al-ishārāt* . . ., ed. Forget [*op. cit.*], p. 68, line 1).

[68] This way of regarding the matter differs (but only slightly) from that of my note on " Some Arabic Technical Terms of Syllogistic Logic and their Greek Originals," *Journal of the American Oriental Society*, vol. 82 (1962), pp. 203–204.

syllogism viewed from the orthodox Aristotelian standpoint.[69] It would be the number of modes of *systasis* of syllogistic *technai* that would represent the crucial factor. This consideration would serve to make a large part of the recent discussions of the matter—in so far as they rely solely or primarily upon the three standard *schēmata* of Galen's *Eisagōgē dialektikē* (and, as we now know, of his other logical works as well)—quite beside the point.[70]

*   *   *

Appendix

This appendix will offer a few scraps of textual evidence that *ṣanʿah* and *banāʾ* is sometimes used to mean syllogism (in the sense of " Galenian " two-premiss-cum-conclusion syllogism) in Arabic logic texts of the earlier period.

(1) In the logic-chapter of the encyclopedia *Keys to the Sciences* (*Mafātīḥ al-ʿulūm*)[71] of the Persian scholar Muḥammad ibn Aḥmad al-Khwārizmī (d. ca. 995) we read: " A ' union ' (*jāmiʿah = symplokē*) exists in a ' connection ' (*qarīnah = syzygia*) and the conclusion when they are united [syllogistically in their terms], and it is also called a *ṣanʿah* ; and its name in Greek is *sūlūjismūs*, i.e., syllogism " (*al-jāmiʿah fī 'l-qarīnah wa-'l-natījah idha jumiʿtān wa-yusammī aiḍān al-ṣanʿah wa-ismihā bi-'l-yūnāniyyah sūlūjismūs ai al-qiyās*). (P. 147 of van Vloten's edition.)

(2) In the section on Aristotle in al-Yaʿqūbī's *Universal History*[72] we read : " When two premisses are taken together with their conclusion it is called a *ṣanʿah* " (*wa-idhā kānat muqaddamāt wa-natījah-hā maʿ-hā summī ṣanʿah* [Houtsma points this as *ṣīghah*]).

(3) As notes above, Avicenna discussed " the inverse of the first (figure) " not as yet another " figure " (*shakl*) but as a " syllogistic construction" (*ibānah qiyāsiyyah*). In his poem on logic (ed. A. Schmölders, Paris, 1836) he also equates *shakl* with *banāʾ* (see p. 129).

As I construe the matter, (1) and (2)—or rather their common source, probably al-Kindī (d. 873)—mirror an originally Greek conception of the syllogism as a complex of two premisses *with the*

---

[69] It should be noted that in his *Eisagōgē dialektikē*, Galen when defining the syllogistic figures (in § vii) treats the syllogism on the two-premisses-only conception, but ultimately shifts (in § xiii)—after the question of which syllogisms are valid in which figures has been settled—to treating syllogisms on the two-premisses-plus-conclusion conception.

[70] Although we have spoken here of Galen's " invention " of the fourth figure, we recognize that one cannot rule out the possibility that Galen took over from Stoic sources conceivably even this figure itself, but in any case very probably the concept of syllogism that goes with it.

[71] Ed. G. van Vloten (Leiden, 1895).

[72] Ed. M. Th. Houtsma, vol. 1 (Leiden, 1883).

conclusion in such a way as to have four modes of construction, and not the standard Aristotelian three.

It is important to distinguish the sense of *ṣanʿah* = *technē* here at issue from another, viz., that of the " syllogistic arts "—as demonstration, topics, rhetoric, sophistics, and poetics came to be called because syllogisms were supposed to be used for reasoning in these fields.[73]

9. *Retrospect*

By way of review it seems appropriate to restate some of the principal theses of our discussion that relate to the bearing of Arabic sources upon the history of the fourth syllogistic figure. (i) Averroes' report that Galen taught the fourth figure derives—and we can say this with virtually complete assurance—from Abū Naṣr al-Fārābī. (ii) In al-Fārābī's time and place, the available information regarding Galen's logical work was such that it is altogether incredible that any mistake in the matter could have arisen. (iii) Averroes' report, when viewed in context, is no longer an isolated and puzzling datum of dubious merits ; it is the reflection of a continuing Arabic tradition of syllogistic teaching, a tradition that can be traced back to its roots in such a way that its authenticity is beyond doubt. Moreover, (iv) we find ample indications in Arabic discussions of the fourth figure to justify us in refusing to give much weight to the fact that in Galen's *Eisagōgē dialektikē* we meet only the three standard Aristotelian *schēmata*. Finally, (v) we obtain from the data such an account of Galen's " advocacy " of a fourth " figure " as to constitute a highly plausible basis for the complete silence we find in all major logical texts of later antiquity with respect to a fourth Galenian figure. These considerations plausibly result in a vindication of the traditional view of Galen as the originator of the fourth figure. They suggest the view that Galen, starting with a variant (and probably Stoic) conception of the nature of a syllogism as involving an explicit conclusion, arrived at a correspondingly variant concept of a syllogistic " figure ", inevitably giving rise to the four familiar figures.

But this position is not too far removed from that of Lukasiewicz. Galen did not teach four " figures " in the sense of Aristotelian *schēmata*, but (rightly) held to the usual three. However, he did doubtless teach

[73] On the syllogistic arts see Steinschneider, *Al-Fārābī* (*op. cit*), pp. 14–18 ; and also N. Rescher, *Al-Fārābī's Short Commentary on Aristotle's " Prior Analytics "* (*op. cit.*), pp. 124, 131.

four " figures " in another context : specifically, in the sense of four modes of *systasis* of the (modern) premisses-cum-conclusion syllogism (thus advocating the concept of four syllogistic figures in exactly the way in which they are taught in college classrooms today). The point at which Lukasiewicz and the Anonymous Scholiast are undoubtedly wrong is in thinking that whatever Galen might have said about compound syllogisms has anything to do with the matter.

*　　*　　*

In concluding this phase of our inquiry one final consideration deserves to be stressed. It is, after all, a rather minor matter for the history of logic to settle the question of whether Galen did or did not invent the fourth figure. The significant feature of the present discussion seems, therefore, to lie not so much in its positive findings about Galen and the fourth figure, as in its affording one small illustration of a more important and far-reaching fact : the largely unexploited potential of Arabic materials as a source of a new insight into the later stages of the history of Greek logic.

Chapter II

THE FOURTH FIGURE IN THE WEST

1. *The Concept of Figure in Aristotle and its Exegesis*

This is not the place to attempt a full-scale study of Aristotle's own conception of syllogistic figure. The authorities differ, and any attempt to settle the matter taking proper account of all the manifold considerations that have been adduced would be very long and complex.[1] Surface impressions notwithstanding, there is substantial justice in H. Maier's observation that " The question of the principle on the basis of which the three Aristotelian figures are distinguished is one of the most difficult questions with which Aristotelian logic confronts an interpreter ".[2] All we can do here is to give a short description of the major alternatives, and to indicate in a dogmatically brief way where our own preference lies :

Conception No. 1

The primary basis for the distinction of the syllogistic figures resides in the *extension* or inclusiveness of the terms involved in a syllogism. This works in such a way that the distinction between a major and a

---

[1] The principal literature of the subject is to be found in the following works : Adolf Trendelenburg, *Logische Untersuchungen* (1st ed., Berlin, 1840 : 2d ed., 1862 ; 3rd ed., 1870 ; photoreprinted, Hildesheim, 1964). Carl Prantl, *Geschichte der Logik im Abendlande*, vol. I (Leipzig, 1855 ; photoreprinted, Graz, 1955). Friederich Ueberweg, *System der Logik* (1st ed., Bonn, 1857 ; 5th ed., 1882). Heinrich Maier, *Die Syllogistik des Aristoteles* (Tübingen, 1896 ; 2d ed., Leipzig, 1936). W. D. Ross, *Aristotle's Prior and Posterior Analytics* (Oxford, 1949). Jan Lukasiewicz, *Aristotle's Syllogistic* (Oxford, 1951 ; 2d ed., 1957). Günther Patzig, *Die Aristotelische Syllogistik* (Göttingen, 1959 ; Abhandlungen der Akademie der Wissenschaften in G., Philologisch-historische Klasse, Dritte Folge, Nr. 42). W. and M. Kneale, *The Development of Logic* (Oxford, 1962).

[2] *Die Syllogistik des Aristoteles* (*op. cit.*), vol. II, part 1, p. 48, notes.

minor term is a secondary and not a fundamental issue.[3] (Nor is reference to the conclusion needed for this distinction.) Three—and only three—possible figures come about according as the middle (i.e., shared) term is :

(1) lesser in extension than one of the two extreme (i.e., non-shared terms and greater than another,
(2) greater than both extremes, and
(3) lesser than both extremes.

On this view three and only three figures are possible—there is no question of a fourth.

This construction of the matter was imputed to Aristotle historically—and was also held to be substantively correct—by most medieval Scholastics,[4] by many or most modern Thomistic logicians, by the many late nineteenth century German logicians (pre-eminently A. Trendelenburg [5]) by many English logicians,[6] and—at one time—by W. D. Ross.[7] A recent attempt to support a refurbished version of Trendelenburg's position is found in Heinrich Maier's work *Die Syllogistik der Aristoteles (op. cit.)*.[8]

[3] This question has been a bone of contention since antiquity. Cf. I. Madkour, *L'Organon d'Aristote dans le monde arabe* (Paris, 1934), pp. 205–206.

[4] See e.g., *Albertus Magnus, Commentaria in Priorum Analyticorum*, bk. I, tract II, ch. ii. The matter is put with exactness and precision by William of Shyreswood : . . . *figura provenit ex dispositione terminorum. Non autem possunt pluribus modes variari nisi tribus modis scilicet quod medium sit subiectum in una propositione et praedicatum in alia aut praedicatum in utraque aut subjectum in utraque. Et ideo sunt tantum tres figurae. Prima, quando medium subicitur in una et predicatur in altera. Secunda, quando predicatur in utraque. Tertia, quando subicitur in utraque.* (M. Grabmann, " *Die ' Introductiones in logicam ' des Wilhelm von Shyreswood,*" *Sitzungsberichte der Bayerischen Akademie der Wissenschaften* (Philosophisch-historische Abteilung), 1937 (Heft 10) ; p. 51 : 21–29.)

[5] His position is concisely outlined—and ably contested—by F. Ueberweg, *System der Logik (op. cit.)*, pp. 332–335.

[6] One instance is H. L. Mansel (in his edition of H. Aldrich's *Artis logicae rudimenta* [*op. cit.*], p. 75, notes) : " Aristotle acknowledges only three figures ; looking rather to the extension of the middle term, as compared with the other two, than to its position in the two premises." (Mansel here follows Trendelenburg.)

[7] *Aristotle* (Oxford, 1923), ch. ii. Cf. also O. Hamelin, *Le système d'Aristote* (Paris, 1920 ; 2d ed., 1931), p. 185.

[8] Regarding this I must cite the discussion of Jan Lukasiewicz (*Aristotle's Syllogistic* [*op. cit.*]) :

[Maier's section] on the syllogistic figures generally and the fourth figure in particular is in my opinion one of the most obscure chapters of his laborious but unfortunate book. Maier writes that two opinions of the criterion for the syllogistic figures stand opposed to each other : one (especially Ueberweg) sees this criterion in the position of the middle term as subject or predicate, the other (especially Trendelenburg) sees it in the extensional relations of the middle term to the extremes. It is not yet settled, Maier says, which of these opinions is right (*op. cit.*, vol. iia, p. 48, n. 1). He adopts the second as his own . . . . (P. 36)
Lukasiewicz goes on to criticize Maier at some length (pp. 36–38), accusing him of reaching " the peak . . . of logical absurdity."

Conception No. 2

The distinction between the major and minor terms is the primary basis. This distinction is drawn on the basis of *the role of the extreme terms in the conclusion* : major term = predicate of the conclusion ; minor term = subject of the conclusion. This underwrites a distinction between a major and a minor premiss. Four possible syllogistic figures result :

	The predicate of the conclusion is predicate of its (i.e., the major) premiss	The subject of the conclusion is subject of its (i.e., the minor) premiss
(1)	yes	yes
(2)	yes	no
(3)	no	yes
(4)	no	no

On this view, four syllogistic figures are theoretically inevitable, and it has to be argued that Aristotle went on to dismiss the fourth figure on grounds not of formal but of substantive considerations (it is unnatural, etc.). Whatever its *substantive* demerits, the fourth figure exists non-redundantly and indispensably on this view.

That this conception of the figures is the logically correct one was— it is here contended—the teaching of Galen (with the qualification introduced above). The conception is met with in Avicenna [9] and in many Arabic logicians after him, including Averroes.[10] It was introduced in Europe in the Renaissance, was taught by Arnauld in the *Port-Royal Logic*, accepted by Leibniz, and is in fact the view held by most modern logicians.[11] The view that this conception was historically that of Aristotle himself has the weighty backing of Jan Lukasiewicz [12] and of so eminent an authority as W. D. Ross,[13] although the interpretation demands that Aristotle be charged with a mistake, blind-spot, oversight (or what you will) that prevented him from recognizing the fourth figure arising inescapably from the concept of figure at issue.

[9] A. M. Goichon (ed.), *Ibn Sīnā : Livre des directives et remarques* (Beirut and Paris, 1951), pp. 197–198. Cf. I. Madkour, *L'Organon d'Aristote dans le monde arabe* (*op. cit.*), p. 206.

[10] *Aristotelis Opera cum Averrois Commentariis*, vol. I (Venice, 1562 ; photoreprinted Frankfurt am Main, 1962), p. 8a, col. 2 of the middle commentary on *Anal. Pr.* (*Priorum Resolutiorum*).

[11] See, for example, the definition of figure in A. Lalande, *Vocabulaire technique et critique de la philosophie* (Paris, 1925 and later) s.v. *figure*.

[12] *Aristotle's Syllogistic* (*op. cit.*), p. 23.

[13] *Aristotle's Prior and Posterior Analytics* (Oxford, 1949), pp. 34–35. In his earlier book on *Aristotle* (Oxford, 1929), however, Ross endorsed Conception No. 1.

Conception No. 3

The distinction between the major and minor premisses (not terms!) is the primary basis. This distinction is drawn on the basis of the *order of occurrence* of the two premisses in the statement of the syllogism: major premiss = first-stated premiss; minor premiss = second-stated premiss (in Aristotle himself presumably the reverse). (Again, no reference to the conclusion is needed for this distinction.) Four syllogistic figures can now be distinguished, according to the role of the middle term in the two premisses:

	In the major premiss the middle term is	*In the minor premiss the middle term is*
(1)	subject	predicate
(2)	predicate	predicate
(3)	subject	subject
(4)	predicate	subject

On this view, four syllogistic figures are theoretically inevitable. However, the fourth figure is now redundant and dispensable, being simply the first with interchanged premisses. Most fifteenth century Latin logicians held this view and it survived at least until Pierre Gassendi in the seventeenth century.[14] (I know of no later supporter of the position.[15])

Conception No. 4

The distinction between the figures is itself the primary basis (and that between major and minor terms and/or premisses supervenes as secondary and derivative). The starting point is a pair of (initially) wholly undifferentiated premisses viewed in the context of the " syllogistic question " of what—if anything—follows from them. (There is thus—as in the case of Conceptions No.'s 1 and 3, and unlike No. 2—no reference to the conclusion.) Three—and only three—possible figures result, according as the middle term is:

(1) subject in one premiss and predicate in the other
(2) predicate in both premisses
(3) subject in both premisses

[14] See p. 34 below.
[15] The question of the proper order of the premisses in the appropriate statement of a syllogism (e.g., major or minor first?) has a long and complex history into which we cannot enter here. Interesting details can be found *passim* in C. Prantl's *Geschichte der Logik im Abendlande* (e.g., vol. I, pp. 587–588), but see also H. Hallam, *Introduction to the Literature of Europe* (American ed., 4 vols. N.Y., 1874), vol. III, pt. III, ch. iii, sect. 151.

On this view three and only three figures are possible—there is no question of a fourth. A distinction between major and minor terms and/or premisses does not come about until after the question of figure has once been settled.

This conception was imputed to Aristotle by Theophrastus,[16] by Alexander of Aphrodisias,[17] by Galen (with the qualifications introduced above) and indeed by most of the logicians of antiquity,[18] and by some of the Arabic logicians (e.g., al-Fārābī and Abū 'l-Barakāt ibn Malkā),[19] and by various Latin medievals (e.g., Abailard).[20] In modern times it has been regarded as the authentically Aristotelian position by A. de Morgan,[21] F. Ueberweg,[22] and more recently apparently also by Mrs. Kneale.[23] According to our own view, it is

[16] Alexander, 69 : 27.

[17] Alexander, 258 : 17 (ad I, 23) and 349 : 5 (ad I, 32). Cf. Lukasiewicz, *Aristotle's Syllogistic* (*op. cit.*), p. 27.

[18] Cf. C. Prantl, *Geschichte der Logik im Abendlande*, vol. I (*op. cit.*), p. 588.

[19] For the former see N. Rescher (tr.), *Al-Fārābī's Short Commentary on Aristotle's " Prior Analytics "* (Pittsburgh, 1963), p. 62. The latter was dealt with in Section 7 above. Ibn al-Ṣalāḥ (as we shall see below) is also perfectly clear as to the distinction between Conception No. 4 (which, however, he does not attribute to Aristotle or al-Fārābī, but only to an anonymous " opponent ") and Conception No. 2 (which he accepts as correct).

[20] See L. Minio-Paluello, *Twelfth Century Logic*, vol. II (Rome, 1958), p. 9

[21] " A little consideration will show the reader that the earlier Aristotelians were wiser than the later ones in this matter. Consider the first and fourth figures as coincident, and the arbitrary notion of arrangement by major and minor vanishes. It was not till this mere matter of discipline was made an article of faith that the fourth figure had any ground of secession from the first." *Formal Logic* (London, 1847), p. 153.

[22] It cannot go without note that F. Ueberweg, clearly recognizing this conception of figure as one that gives rise to the three orthodox figures in a natural way (*System der Logik* [*op. cit.*], p. 320), goes on to impute this conception to Aristotle (*ibid.*, pp. 333, 337). In historic justice, we must place on record our conviction that Ueberweg's discussion of the syllogistic figures is a magisterial one to which subsequent logicians and historians of logic have—to their own detriment—failed to accord sufficient attention. Even Ueberweg's opponent A. Trendelenburg was prepared to recognize the strength of his case (*Logische Untersuchungen*, vol. II [3rd ed., Leipzig, 1870 ; photoreprinted, Hildesheim, 1964], p. 344.

[23] *The Development of Logic* (*op. cit.*), p. 68. The verbal characterization conforms entirely to our Conception No. 4, although the diagrams given prejudice the issue by specifying a fixed order of the extreme terms in the conclusion. However, substantial merit attaches to Mrs. Kneale's suggestion (pp. 71–72) that Aristotle may in usual practice have represented a syllogism as a group of three letters (for example, *ABC*), with each pair (*AB*, *BC*, *AC*) representing a categorical proposition, and then letting the terms A, B, C serve as major (M), minor (m) and middle (μ) in the order : $M\mu m$ (first figure), $\mu M m$ (second figure), and $M m \mu$ (third figure). (Given the understanding that M must precede m—and introducing a fourth figure amounts to dropping this restriction—these are the only figures that can arise.) This suggestion of the Kneales is developed in detail in Lynn E. Rose, " Aristotle's Syllogistic and the Fourth Figure," *Mind*, vol. 74 (1965), pp. 382–389.

A much more complicated view which is, in effect, a mixture of Conception No.'s 1

the correct interpretation of Aristotle's position on the question of the syllogistic figures.[24]

*   *   *

The principal considerations that militate in favor of an interpretation of the concept of figure in *Prior Analytics* along the lines of Conception No. 4 are :

(1) Aristotle takes the pair-of-premisses-plus-question rather than the pair-of-premisses-cum-conclusion view of the syllogism as his starting point.

(2) Aristotle's distinction of the figure does not require any reference to the conclusion to effect a distinction between the premisses.

(3) Aristotle's characterizations of the figures are exactly as one would expect on this fourth conception of the figures.

*   *   *

The principal considerations that militate against the other three conceptions are as follows :

Conception No. 1

Aristotle does not, in fact, take term-extension relationships as his starting point in distinguishing the figures. As M. Kneale rightly remarks : " Only in his [Aristotle's] definitions for the first figure is there any reference to the comparative extension of the application of the terms ".[25] And if he is held to have done so, a host of difficulties can be laid at his door, e.g., how could one possibly settle questions of term-inclusiveness on the basis of schematic letters (variables) instead of concrete terms ? In point of fact, this extensional view makes a complete hash of the concept of syllogistic figure.[26]

and 4—specifically that Aristotle viewed the first syllogistic figure from the standpoint of No. 1 and the second and third from that of No. 4—has been held by various authorities. (It is adumbrated, for example, by I. Madkour, *L'Organon d'Aristote dans le monde arabe* [Paris, 1934], pp. 205–207.) Recently a position of this type has been elaborately and ably defended by Günther Patzig, *Die Aristotelische Syllogistik (op. cit.).*

[24] Our enumeration of alternative conceptions of the matter bypasses entirely some wholly idiosyncratic ideas, such as that of J. H. von Kirchmann, who maintains " Da indess die letze Figur [d.h. die echt galenische] sich mehr der Sprache des Lebens insbesondere bei den modernen Sprachen anpasst, so hat man diese galenische Figur zur ersten Figur erhoben und sonderbarer Weise fur die erklärt, welche Aristoteles aufgestellt habe." (*Erläuterungen zu den ersten Analytiken des Aristoteles* [Leipzig, 1877], p. 31.)

[25] W. and M. Kneale, *The Development of Logic (op. cit.),* p. 69.

[26] See pp. 45–47 above. See also F. Ueberweg, *System der Logik (op. cit.),* p. 333 ; G. Patzig, *Die Aristotelische Syllogistik (op. cit.),* pp. 123 ff. ; and W. and M. Kneale, *The Development of Logic (op. cit.),* p. 69.

Conception No. 2

This again has the serious disadvantage of regarding the distinction of major and minor terms as basic. Furthermore—and perhaps even more seriously—it holds that the distinction is to be drawn on the basis of the role of the extreme terms in the conclusion. But this contention is false to Aristotle's own procedure, and it represents a point of view that did not enter the Aristotelian tradition before Philoponus.

Conception No. 3

While this conception of syllogistic figure is plausible and attractive enough of itself, it is entirely without merit as an interpretation of Aristotle, for whom the order of statement of the premisses of a syllogism is by no means a fundamental but a highly derivative matter. (The " canonical " ordering of a syllogism minor-major [-conclusion] is not to be settled until *after* (i) the figure has been determined, and (ii) the major and minor terms—and thus the corresponding premisses—have been discriminated.)

*   *   *

According to our view, then, Aristotle's own view of syllogistic figure was that of Conception No. 4. For him the indirect moods of the first figure would then have been—as indeed they were—simply first-figure syllogisms, and of course valid ones, albeit of a somewhat strained and nonstandard variety.

*   *   *

A most eloquent and formidable opponent of this view has recently come to the fore in J. Lukasiewicz. It is necessary to consider his position at some length. Lukasiewicz writes :

> The position of the middle term as subject or predicate of the premisses is the principle by which Aristotle divides the syllogistic moods into figures. Aristotle says explicitly that we shall recognize the figure by the position of the middle term (*An. Pr.* I, 32 ; 47b 13). In the first figure the middle term is the subject of *the major term* and the predicate of *the minor term*, in the second figure it is the predicate, and in the last figure the subject, of both the other terms. Aristotle, however, is mistaken when he says that every syllogism must be in one of these three figures. There is a fourth possibility, viz. that the middle term is the predicate of the major term and the subject of the minor term. Moods of this kind are now spoken of as belonging to the fourth figure. (*Op. cit.*, p. 23.)

This way of putting the matter comes within a hair's breath of our own. Replace here the two italicized (by us) references to *specific* terms by the indefinite " one of the extreme terms ", and at once Lukasiewicz's " fourth possibility " disappears and Aristotle's mistake along with it. Lukasiewicz is himself aware of this, for he writes :

> It follows from these facts that Aristotle knows and accepts all the [valid] moods of the fourth figure. This must be emphasized against the opinion of some philosophers that he rejected these moods. Such a rejection would be a logical error which cannot be imputed to Aristotle. His only mistake is the omission of these moods in the systematic division of the syllogisms. We do not know why he did so. . . . Theophrastus, indeed, found for the moods of the fourth figure which are " homeless " in Aristotle's system a place among the moods of the first figure. For this purpose he had to introduce a slight modification into the Aristotelian definition of the first figure. Instead of saying that in the first figure the middle term is the subject of the major and the predicate of the minor, as Aristotle does (*An. Pr.* I, 23 ; 40b 30 and 41a 13), he said generally that in the first figure the middle term is the subject of one premiss and the predicate of another. Alexander repeats this definition (258 : 15 *ad* I, 23), which probably comes from Theophrastus, and seems not to see that it differs from the Aristotelian description of the first figure. The correction of Theophrastus is as good a solution of the problem of the syllogistic figures as the addition of a new figure. (*Op. cit.*, pp. 27–28.)

Lukasiewicz's eloquently articulated position rests on a foundation of sand. The Aristotelian texts he cites do not support his interpretation in any decisive or unequivocal way, and there is no reason to believe that Theophrastus thought that the extra first figure moods were left " homeless " by Aristotle rather than merely slighted by him. Instead, there is every reason to believe that Theophrastus' characterization of the syllogistic figures represents an *exposition* of Aristotle's position rather than a *modification* of it. And when Alexander agrees with Theophrastus, why must we take this to show that he " seems not to see that it differs from Aristotle's description of the first figure " rather than as a meaningful indication that the best Aristotelians of antiquity had got the Master's teaching in this matter aright ?

*   *   *

In brief summary, the main stages in the development of the conception of syllogistic figure in antiquity after Aristotle were as follows :

Aristotle's pupils Theophrastus (certainly) and Eudemus (perhaps also) gathered up the five nonstandard syllogisms of the first figure—whose existence and validity are already recognized by Aristotle—and grouped them together, according them an explicit, systematic recognition as the fifth to ninth modes of first figure syllogisms (in the order that was to become canonical : 5. Bramatip, 6. Calemes, 7. Dimatis, 8. Fesapo, 9. Fresison). They may have termed these the " reverse " (*kata anaklasin ; per refractionem* in Boethius and the Medieval Latin) modes of the first figure, and in any case later writers did so.[27] This approach prevailed universally (or almost so) throughout antiquity.

The later Peripatetics made certain technical distinctions and classifications that removed some uncertainties in Aristotle's own discussions. Especially important is : (1) The distinction (first found in Alexander of Aphrodisias) between the premisses-only " syllogism " (*zyzygia*) and the premisses-cum-conclusion " syllogism " (*symplokē*). (2) The policy (found, e.g., in Philoponus, and adopted by virtually all medieval and modern writers [28]) of defining the major and middle terms with respect to their role in the conclusion.[29] As we have already observed, this second position points forcibly in the direction of a fourth syllogistic figure—although Philoponus himself did not travel this road.

Finally, there is unequivocal evidence that the *per refractionem* moods of the first figure were taken by some (few and obscure) logicians to represent a separate, fourth figure no later than the sixth century and very likely before [30] —certainly so on our view regarding Galen.

2. *A Brief Account of the History of the Fourth Figure in Western Logic After Antiquity*

Writing of the attitude toward the fourth figure in medieval logic in the Latin West, I. M. Bochenski comments :

> We know of no scholastic logical text in Latin where the fourth figure in the modern sense can be found, though all logicians of the period develop the " indirect moods of the first ".[31]

[27] For evidence and texts see C. Prantl, *Geschichte der Logik im Abendlande (op. cit.)*, vol. I, pp. 365–368. Also, there is a good briefer discussion in F. Ueberweg, *System der Logik (op. cit.)*, pp. 339–340.

[28] Philoponus, *In Aristotelis Analytica Priora Commentaria*, ed. M. Wallies (Berlin, 1905), p. 67. See W. and M. Kneale, *The Development of Logic (op. cit.)*, p. 71, where the relevant passage is translated and discussed, and compare p. 70, where it is noted that this view was already suggested by Alexander of Aphrodisias (*In Aristotelis Analyticorum Priorum Librum I Commentarium*, ed. M. Wallies [Berlin, 1883], p. 75).

[29] Although condemned by Pacius (*ad Anal. Pr.* I, 7) as inapplicable to the indirect moods—which led Mansel (in his edition of Aldrich's *Artis logicae rudimenta*, p. 67, notes) to comment irritably that in such a matter " the indirect moods may, without loss, be dispensed with."

[30] J. Lukasiewicz, *Aristotle's Syllogistic (op. cit.)*, p. 41. Cf. L. M. de Rijk (ed.), *Petrus Abaelardus Dialectica* (Assen, 1956), p. lxiv.

[31] I. M. Bochenski, *A History of Formal Logic* (English tr. by I. Thomas ; Notre Dame, 1961), p. 216.

As W. Kneale remarks, "It is curious that we have no trace of anyone [in Western logic] who defended the doctrine of four figures before the end of the Middle Ages ".[32] The mnemonics of the Barbara-Celarent type were generally known by about 1275 or somewhat earlier, but of course envisaged no fourth figure but an indirect first : [33]

    I. Barbara, Celarent, Darii, Ferion
    (I). Baralipton, Celantes, Dabitis, Fapesmo, Frisesomorum
    II. Cesare, Camestres, Festino, Baroco
    III. Darapti, Felapton, Disamis, Datisi, Bocardo, Ferison

The later form of these mnemonics, dropping (I) and adding

    IV. Bamalip, Calemes, Dimatis, Fesapo, Fresison,

or in most later writers

    IV. Bramantip, Camenes, Dimaris, Fesapo, Fresison

has not been traced back further than the *Institutio logicae* of John Wallis (Oxford, 1687). (Wallis, gave the two sets of mnemonics, i.e., those for the fourth figure as well as those for the indirect first.[34] The fourth-figure mnemonics were popularized in the *Artis logicae rudimenta* [or *compendium*] of Henry Aldrich [Oxford, 1691].) This conception of three syllogistic figures is found in the works of such early medieval logicians as Peter Abailard (1079–1142), Albert the Great (1193–1280), William of Shyreswood (d. 1249), and continues with later medieval logicians such as William of Ockham (d. 1349), and Paul of Venice (d. 1429).[35] The earliest Medieval Latin argument against the fourth figure, mentioning it by name, that is known to me, occurs in the writings of Lambert of Auxerre (fl. ca. 1250).[36]

---

[32] W. and M. Kneale, *The Development of Logic* (Oxford, 1962), p. 183. The idea that there might be more than the three standard figures " was combatted by all the logicians of the Middle Ages, and began to come into favor only during the Renaissance." (E. Rabier, *Logique* [Paris, 1886], p. 66.)

[33] Thus in Peter of Spain (d. 1277) as cited by Bochenski, *op. cit.*, p. 212. The mnemonics do not occur in Abailard (1079–1142) but as far as we know were first used by William of Shyreswood (d. 1249). See L. M. de Rijk (ed.) *Petrus Abaelardus : Dialectica* (Assen, 1956), p. lxiv, notes.

[34] See J. N. Keynes, *Studies and Exercises in Formal Logic* (*op. cit.*), p. 330, notes.

[35] For Abailard see *Petrus Abaelardus : Dialectica*, ed. L. M. de Rijk (Assen, 1956), p. lxiv. For the rest, see the text-citations given by I. M. Bochenski, *op. cit.*, pp. 216–217.

[36] *Item possit aliquis dicere . . . quod debeat esse quarta figura, in qua medius praedicetur in majori et subiiciatur in minori. Ad hoc dicendum, quod tantum sunt tres figurae syllogismi. . . . Alia figura esse non potest, in qua medium praedicatur de majore extremitate et subiiciatur minori extremitati ; nam secundum illam dispositionem medii oporteret sumere maiorem falsam, si sumeretur universalis, vel oporteret sumere particularem, et tunc non sequeretur conclusio.* Cited in Prantl, *op. cit.*, vol. III, p. 30, n. 121. (Lambert's argument is specious—it shows no more than that a fourth-figure syllogism cannot validly lead to an *A* [universal affirmative] conclusion.) Lambert's argument is echoed frequently in medieval logical texts, e.g., in Duns Scotus (d. 1308 ; see *ibid.*, p. 231), and in Giles of Rome

In the second half of the fifteenth century the fourth figure achieved a more prominent and secure place for itself. Peter of Mantua (fl. ca. 1460–1470) in his *Logica* (Pavia, 1483) recognized the fourth figure and surveyed its valid moods.[37] To Peter Tartaret (fl. ca. 1480), however, belongs the honor of being the first modern European logician to argue for a distinct fourth figure. He held it to have four valid moods of which he said that they *reducuntur ad modos primae figurae per solam transpositionem praemissarum.*[38] The favorable attitude to the fourth figure on the part of these later fifteenth century logicians is not surprising in view of the fact that they adopted an approach which—given their conception of major and minor premisses (and terms)—was perfectly natural and correct.[39] For they defined the major and minor premisses *solely in terms of their order of statement* (major = first-stated, minor = second-stated), without any reference to the conclusion. In this way they arrived at a fourth figure, but one which cannot really be regarded as a genuinely separate figure : it is simply the first figure with the premisses interchanged. Already Ockham (d. 1349) had advanced the essentials of the view :

> *Et non est apponenda quarta figura, quia si medius terminus predicatur in prima propositione* (= the major) *et subiicitur in secunda* (= the minor) *non erit nisi transpositio propositionum positarum in prima figura et ideo non sequitur alia conclusio quam illa quae sequitur ex praemissis dispositis in prima figura* . . .[40]

The Ockhamist view was to become more or less standard in the fifteenth century : A fourth figure can be conceived of, but it is nothing other than the reverse of the first and is—according to most writers—unnatural.[41]

(d. 1316 ; see *ibid.*, p. 264). Lambert's position is certainly anticipated in ch. 5 " *De sufficientia figurarum trium habitarum* " of bk. IV of Albert the Great's *Commentaria in Priorum Analyticorum Liber I*, but Albert does not mention a fourth figure by name.

[37] See Prantl, *op. cit.*, vol. IV, pp. 178–179. After noting that Peter recognized 15 moods as valid for the first figure, 16 for the second, and 18 for the third, Prantl continues : " aber auch für die vierte Figur giebt er in ungenirter Naivetät, ohne mit einem Worte auf die bestehenden Controversen einzugehen, folgende fünfzehn Modi an. . . ."

[38] *Ibid.*, p. 205 ; cf. n. 7 of Chapter III below. Tartaret does, however, go on to state that *Sola transpositio praemissarum non ponit diversitatem figurarum, sed bene transpositio praemissarum cum alia habitudine medii ad extremitates ponit diversitatem figurarum.* Among the writers who follow Tartaret's lead are Jodoc Trutfelder, one of the teachers of Luther (d. 1519 ; see Prantl, *ibid.*, p. 242) and Johann Eck (d. 1543 ; see Prantl, *ibid.*, pp. 286–287). However, Peter Tartaret's following was not restricted to the Protestant orbit, but apparently was especially prominent in the University of Paris. (See the citation from Giorgio Benegno given in Prantl, *ibid.*, p. 290, n. 720.)

[39] See I. M. Bochenski, *A History of Formal Logic* (*op. cit.*), pp. 216–217.

[40] Cited in E. A. Moody, *The Logic of William of Ockham* (London, 1935), p. 212, notes.

[41] Thus also Pierre de la Ramée (1515–1572) : *Petrus Ramus ; Aristotelicae animadversiones* (Paris, 1573 ; photoreprinted Stuttgart–Bad Cannstatt, 1964), p. 62b.

This situation began to alter when—in the wake of the Renaissance—Arabic *logical* texts (especially those of Averroes) came to be generally available in Latin. (The earliest example of a Latin author who attributes the fourth figure to Galen—and thereby gives presumptive evidence of familiarity with Averroes' discussion—is Marsilius of Inghen [d. 1396].[42]) It is not that these texts favored or advocated the fourth figure—they usually did the reverse—but they promulgated a variant conception of syllogistic " figure " that paved the way for a more favorable reception of the fourth. The question of a figure was now no longer simply one hinging upon the *order of listing* of the premisses, but of the arrangemental relationship of their terms to the terms of the conclusion. This laid the basis for a more significant distinction between the syllogistic orderings in the first and fourth figures. This conception of figure was influentially promulgated in Jacob Zabarella's treatise, *De quarta syllogismorum figura*,[43] although Zabarella himself argued the artificiality and superfluity of a fourth figure (following Averroes).[44] Thus, while the basis for a more favorable view of the fourth figure was laid in the Renaissance, the figure itself continued to be downgraded or rejected—as indeed it was by all those Arabic logicians whose writings were accessible.[45]

---

[42] See Prantl, *op. cit.*, vol. IV, p. 98.

[43] *Opera* (Leiden, 1587), pp. 41 ff. ; *Opera logica* (Basel, 1594), cols. 101 ff. Zabarella, 1532–1589 put the matter of a fourth figure as follows : *quod si positione medius sit, nempe de minore extremo praedicetur, & subijciatur majori, oritur figura prima . . . Hac est Aristotelis sententia de numero figurarum. Galenus vero quartam termini medij sedem, proinde quartam figuram inuenisse videtur ; est autem quarta sedes, si medius ponatur minori extremo subiectus in propositione minore, & de maiore praedicatus in propositione maiore.* (Basel ed., col. 103.) On Zabarella's logic generally see Wilhelm Risse, *Die Logik der Neuzeit,* vol. I (Stuttgart–Bad Cannstatt, 1964), pp. 278–290.

[44] Zabarella's earlier compatriot Augustinus Niphus (1473–1546), in his *Super libros Priorum [Analyticorum] Aristotelis commentaria* (Venice, 1554), hewed to same Averroist line later adopted by Zabarella, holding that a fourth syllogistic figure does arise but is unnatural : *Figura . . . quarta, in qua medium de praedicato conclusionis praedicatur et subiecto eiusdem subiicitur, est praeternaturalis, imo de ea ars non loquitur, cum ars imitetur naturam* (26 va.). Quoted from Wilhelm Risse, *Die Logik der Neuzeit,* vol. I (*op. cit.*), p. 224, n. 111. Niphus' younger contemporary Joh. Franc. Burana took a more reactionary stand in his *Super libros Priorum resolutiorum Aristotelis . . . commentaria* (Venice, 1524), refusing to countenance the fourth figure as other than a special case of the first. (W. Risse, *op. cit.*, p. 231.) The standard objection to the fourth figure—found in much the same words in many authors—is that *praemissae in quarta figura nonnisi penes transpositionem differant a praemissis figurae primae* (Olivier of Siena cited in Prantl, *op. cit.*, vol. IV, p. 234 ; compare, e.g., Erasmus Wonsidel, *ibid.*, p. 274). Even the denunciation of Galen becomes standardized : *patet quod Galienus solum multiplicavit verba super Aristotelem et non realiter.* (*Ibid.*, compare p. 249, n. 435 with p. 272, n. 599.)

[45] Zabarella speaks of unidentified *defensores Galeni* or *sectatores Galeni* but these are presumably Arabs (or Jews) mentioned in his sources.

An early instance of recognition of the fourth figure occurs in English logic. Richard Crackenthorpe (1569–1624) first published his *Logicae libri quinque de praedicabilibus* in London in 1622. (There were numerous later editions of this book mostly issued in Oxford.) In this work Crackenthorpe inaugurated the tendency among a part of the English logicians to recognize the fourth figure, by treating it as distinct from the indirect first.[46]

In the *Logica Hamburgensis* of Joachim Jungius [47] the figures are defined in such a way that a fourth figure arises,[48] and it is recognized and dealt with, albeit in a detached and subsidiary way.[49] The fourth spurious figure (*spuria quasi quaedam figura*) is treated as an artificial transposition of the first, its valid moods representing syllogism-like arguments rather than syllogisms proper (*speciem syllogismi Categorici simulant*). The fourth figure is wholly unnatural (*a consueto ratiocinandi usu omnino exsulet*).[50] The approach is on the whole close to that of Zabarella.

The major change came in the second half of the seventeenth century. A particularly important role was played by the *Port Royal Logic* (1662) of Antoine Arnauld.[51] Here the modern standpoint comes to the fore : Major and minor premisses are defined directly with reference to the conclusion, and four distinct figures inevitably result. The late medieval view that the first and fourth figure differ merely by an exchange of the premisses is firmly rejected :

> Those who take as fourth-figure syllogisms, syllogisms in which the major and minor premisses are interchanged are undoubtedly misguided. Such persons would say that a syllogism such as
>> All bodies are divisible
>> <u>All that is divisible is imperfect</u>
>> Therefore, all bodies are imperfect
> is a syllogism in the fourth figure, a figure they accuse Aristotle of not having recognized. I am astonished that [Pierre] Gassendi should have fallen into this error. To take for the major premiss of a syllogism that sentence which is found first in the syllogism and for the minor premiss the second sentence is ridiculous. . . . Rather a syllogism must be taken as a first-figure syllogism if the middle term is the subject of the premiss in which the major term [*defined* as the predicate of the conclusion] occurs and is the predicate of the premiss in which the minor term [i.e., the

---

[46] Cf. H. W. B. Joseph, *An Introduction to Logic (op. cit.)*, p. 284, notes.

[47] Hamburg, 1632 ; reprinted Hamburg, 1962.

[48] See the definitions of the first three figures on pp. 129–135 of the reprint.

[49] *Ibid.*, pp. 187–189.

[50] *Ibid.* See also the editor's note on p. 187.

[51] I cite this work in the English translation of J. Dickoff and P. James—*Antoine Arnauld : The Art of Thinking : Port Royal Logic* (New York, 1964).

subject of the conclusion] occurs. And only those syllogisms are fourth-figure syllogisms in which the middle term is the predicate in the major premiss and the subject of the minor premiss. In this sense we shall use the word " figure ".[52]

From this standpoint four figures are inevitable. And in the light of it, Arnauld's concession to the tradition—the *en passant* remark that " since in the fourth figure the conclusion is obtained in a way both unnatural and when of this mind, Aristotle and his followers did not recognize a fourth figure "[53]—was not a matter of great weight.

Leibniz—and then following him L. Euler [54]—adhered to the *Port Royal Logic's* endorsement of an independent figure.[55] Thus in a letter to C.D. Koch of September 2, 1708, Leibniz wrote :

> *Interim posteriores [sc. ad Aristotelem] quartam figuram non male adjecere, quam Galeno tribuit Averroës, etsi nullum ejus vestigium sit in scriptis Galenicis quae extant. Quos vulgo vocant modos indirectos primae figurae, revera sunt quartae [si modo praemissae transponantur]. Et inepte eos invexere quidam Logici, ut quartam Galenicam vitarent. Sane nuda transpositio praemissarum non mutat figuram, cum semper illa sit major vel minor propositio, in qua major vel minor terminus conclusionis extat, quocunque praemissa ponatur loco. Cum ergo illi modi primae dicti indirecti habeant hoc sensu medium praedicatum in propositione majore, et medium subjectum in propositione minore, haud dubie pertinent ad quartam figuram, non ad primam.[56]*

Leibniz took this position not only in private correspondence, but in his published writings as well.[57]

The fourth figure enters into prominence in English logic in two late seventeenth century Oxford texts : John Wallis, *Institutio logicae ad communes usus accomodata* (Oxoniae, 1687) ; and Henry Aldrich, *Artis logicae compendium* or *Artis logicae rudimenta* (Oxoniae, 1691). Wallis devotes a special chapter to the fourth figure (ch. IX of pt. III), defining it in the modern way and accepting it as natural. He writes that : *Videntur autem mihi consonantius cum ratione loqui, qui hosce modos vocant Directus figurae Quartae, quam figurae primae Indirectos* and goes on to add

---

[52] *Ibid.*, pp. 188–189.
[53] *Ibid.*, p. 188.
[54] *Letters to a German Princess on Different Subjects in Natural Philosophy*, no. 106 (28th February, 1761).
[55] For an interesting critique of the entire *Port-Royal* approach see J. Duval-Jouve, *Traité de logique* (Paris, 1844), p. 306.
[56] *Philosophische Schriften* (ed. C. I. Gerhard), vol. VII, pp. 477–478. Leibniz takes repeated, careful, and favorable cognizance of the fourth figure in his numerous discussions of syllogistic logic, beginning with his 1646 *Dissertatio de Arte Combinatoria* (see *Phil. Schr.*, vol. IV, pp. 51–53).
[57] See, e.g., the *New Essays Concerning Human Understanding*, bk. IV, ch. ii, sect. 1.

that *omnes utiles sunt et non rejiciendi.*[58] Aldrich defines the figures in the modern way so that a fourth is inevitable,[59] he accepts it and treats it in as full detail as the others, but appends the remark :

> *Adverte etiam, quod figura quarta tribus caeteris deterior est ; cum aliis de causis, tum ex hoc praesertim, quod medium dicat de majori, hunc de minori, minorem de medio, h.e. medium nugatorie de seipso.*[60]

Leibniz's disciple Christian Wolff deserted the position of his master regarding the fourth figure. In his smaller German logic-book he dealt only with the first figure,[61] and even in his larger Latin logic-treatise he dealt only with the usual three figures, omitting mention not only of the fourth figure but even the indirect moods of the first.[62] He taught, in the way usual since Appuleius and Boethius, that the first figure is the most natural—resulting immediately from the *dicto de omni et nullo*—and is the *figura perfecta* in terms of which the other two *figurae imperfectae* are established. Wolff, however, went beyond this standard position in maintaining : *syllogismi secundae* ... [*et*] *syllogismi tertiae figurae sunt syllogismi cryptici primae ;* ... *apparet adeo, non opus esse, ut peculiares pro iis figurae constituantur.* Thus the second and third figures are for Wolff without individual merit, but are merely " cryptic " modifications of the first.[63]

---

[58] *Loc. cit.* I have used the 3rd ed. of Wallis' book (Oxford, 1702). Of the Oxford logic-texts of the period from Crackenthorpe to Wallis, I have been able to check only the *Elementa logicae* of Edward Brerewood (Oxford, 1612), the *Aditus ad logicam* of Samuel Smith (Oxford, 1684), and the very popular *Logicae artis compendium* of Robert Sanderson (Oxford, 1615 ; reprinted for over a century). All of these works treat only of the three orthodox figures. Further probing would no doubt shed more light on the fate of the fourth figure during this very active period, for which see W. S. Howell, *Logic and Rhetoric in England : 1500–1700* (Princeton, 1956).

[59] It is here that we find the syllogistic mnemonic *Barbara*, etc., complete to the fourth figure, in modern form. See H. W. B. Joseph, *Introduction to Logic* (*op. cit.*), p. 285, notes, where there is a claim to priority that must—as we saw at the beginning of this section—be yielded to Wallis.

[60] See pp. 89–90 of Aldrich's work in the re-issue of H. L. Mansel (Oxford, 1852 ; 2d ed.) ; I have not used the original edition of Aldrich. Nor have I been able to check some of the logic books of the older class, such as those of Franco Burgersdicius (1590–1636 ; a professor at Leiden, whose *Logic* the young J. S. Mill studied in 1819) and his contemporary Martinus Smiglecius. For these (and other) now obscure logicians of the period, see Wilhelm Risse, *Die Logik der Neuzeit*, vol. I (*op. cit.*), and W. S. Howell, *Logic and Rhetoric in England : 1500–1700* (*op. cit.*).

[61] Friederich Ueberweg, *System der Logik* (5th ed., Bonn, 1882), p. 342.

[62] *Philosophia rationalis sive Logica* (Francofurta et Lipsiae, 1728 ; 2d ed., 1732), §§ 365–397.

[63] *Ibid.*, §§ 385, 397. See also Christian August Crusius, *Weg zur Gewissheit und Zuverlässigkeit der menschlichen Erkenntnis* (Leipzig, 1747 ; 2d ed. 1762), § 353 (p. 598 of the 1st ed.). We read already in the *Institutiones dialecticae* of Cunradus Theodoricus Dietericus (Gissae, 1609 and later) : *Tribus his vulgatis figuris Galenus ejusque sectatores adjiciunt quartam, in qua medius terminus praedicatur de Majori et subjicitur Minori. Verum absque ulla manifesta necessitate. 1. enim ei non competit definitio Syllogismi legitimaque medii*

It is but a small step from Wolff's position to that of Kant's *Die falsche Spitzfindigkeit der vier syllogistischen Figuren erwiesen* (1762) : rationally pure inference is possible only in the first figure. Only impure or hybrid reasonings (*ratiocinia hybrida*) are possible in the other figures, which draw their inferential force (*vis consequentiae*) from the first. A fourth-figure syllogism :

> . . . contains indeed the matter, but not the form of our reasoning, and it is not at all a ratiocination according to the logical order in which alone the division of the four figures is possible . . . [A fourth figure syllogism may be legitimate but] is not distinguished from one in the first figure by a difference in the place of the middle term, but only by this, that the order of the premisses has been changed, and in the conclusion the order of the extremes. But this does not constitute an alteration in the figure. There is an error of this kind in Crusius' *Logic* in the place referred to, where the author believes that by taking the liberty of changing the order of the premisses he draws the conclusion in the fourth figure, and that more naturally. It is a pity to see the trouble that an able man takes trying to improve a useless thing. The only useful thing one can do with it is to annihilate it.[64]

J. H. Lambert, on the other hand, in his *Neues Organon* (Leipzig, 1764) regards the four figures as being of equal rank. If the first figure rests on the *Dictum de omni et nullo*, the fourth rests on the *Dictum de reciproco* :

> Wenn kein *M*, *B* ist ; so ist auch kein B dieses oder jenes M ; wenn C dieses oder jenes B ist, oder nicht ist ; so giebt es B, die C sind, oder nicht sind.[65]

In Isaac Watts' *Logick* (pt. III, ch. ii, sect. 3), first published in London in 1725 and reissued in numerous editions, we find that the fourth figure is cursorily dismissed in a manner typical of a certain class of English logic texts down to the present century :

> There is also a *fourth Figure*, wherein the middle Term is predicated in the major Proposition, and subjected in the minor : But this is a very indirect and oblique Manner of concluding, and is never used in the Sciences, nor in human Life, and therefore I call it useless.—Some Logicians will allow it to be nothing else but a mere Inversion of the first

---

cum quaestione dispositio. Minor enim terminus praeponitur majori. 2. *Eadem est cum prima figura cum sit ejus quasi crypsis. Licet enim subjectum in propositione et praedicatum in assumptione disponi videatur, reverâ tamen partes sunt per crypsin inversae, et ad primam Figuram reducendae.* (Pp. 336–337 of the 1613 ed., quoted from R. W. Meyer [ed.], *J. Jungii Logica Hamburgiensis* [Hamburg, 1962], p. 187, notes.) Cf. also the passage quoted in W. Risse, *Die Logik der Neuzeit*, vol. I (*op. cit.*), p. 463, n. 118. The conception of *crypsis* is developed at considerable length by Jungius, *op. cit.*, bk. II, ch. ii.

[64] Tr. T. K. Abbott, Kant's *Introduction to Logic* (London, 1885), pp. 66–67. On Crusius see the preceding footnote.

[65] *Op. cit.*, § 232 ; see the entire context §§ 218–232.

Figure ; the Moods of it, (*viz.*) *Baralipton*, or *Barbari, Calentes, Dibatis, Fespamo, Fresisom*, are not worthy to be explained by one Example.[66]

We find essentially the same position—generally with greater attention to details—held in the following works (among many others, generally less influential ones) : [67]

Richard Whately, *Elements of Logic* (London, 1825 ; 9th ed., 1848). [See bk. II, ch. iii, sect. 4. Whately recognizes but disparages the fourth figure.]

J. S. Mill, *A System of Logic* (2 vols., London, 1843). [See bk. II, ch. ii, sect. 1. Mill here follows Whately, but also cites favorably J. H. Lambert's *Neues Organon.*]

W. H. Karslake, *Aids to the Study of Logic* (2 vols., Oxford, 1851). [See vol. I, pp. 74–75.]

Francis Bowen, *Treatise on Logic* (Cambridge, Mass., 1864 ; 10th ed. 1874). [See p. 192 of the 10th ed. of this enormously popular American work.]

W. Stanley Jevons, *Elementary Lessons in Logic* (1st ed., London, 1870 ; 22d edition, 1903 ; American ed., New York, 1920). [See pp. 147–148 of the American ed.]

H. W. B. Joseph, *An Introduction to Logic* (Oxford, 1906 ; 2d edition, 1916). [See pp. 258–259, 280–286.]

A. N. Prior, *Formal Logic* (Oxford, 1955). [See pp. 111–114.]

As of the last half of the nineteenth century, a sector of English logic tended—under the initial impetus of persons influenced by symbolic logic—to take a more favorable view of the fourth figure. The pioneers were George Boole [68] and Augustus de Morgan,[69] both of whom treated the four figures as on a par. Many later writers on syllogistic logic reacted to such influences by according to the fourth figure a place on more or less the same plane with the second and third. Among the more significant instances are :

J. N. Keynes, *Studies and Exercises in Formal Logic* (London, 1884 ; 4th ed., 1906). [See pp. 328–331 of the 4th ed.]

J. Welton, *A Manual of Logic* (2 vols., London, 1891 ; 2d ed., 1896). [See vol. I, pp. 310–311, 314, 337–340 of the 2d ed.]

W. E. Johnson, *Logic* (Pt. I, Cambridge, 1921 ; Pt. II, Cambridge, 1922 ; Pt. III, Cambridge, 1924). [See Pt. II, ch. 20, sects. 9–10.]

---

[66] Watts here followed (and in general relies heavily upon) the logic-treatises of John Wallis and Henry Aldrich.

[67] The list omits that stormy Scotchman, Sir William Hamilton. He will hear nothing about a fourth figure (see his essay " Of Syllogism, its Kinds, Canons, Notations, etc.," printed as Appendix II to his *Discussions on Philosophy and Literature* [London, 1852]).

[68] *The Mathematical Analysis of Logic* (London, 1847 ; photoreprinted, New York, 1948), pp. 31–47.

[69] *Formal Logic* (London, 1847 ; reprinted, London, 1946), pp. 17–18 and 132–136 of the 1st ed.

German logicians of the first half of the nineteenth century generally followed Kant's views on the syllogism at least as far as dismissing the fourth figure. Hegel [70] and J. F. Herbart [71] disparage the figure. Adolf Trendelenburg concludes his discussion of the matter with the remark : " Die ganze vierte Figur ist demnach ein künstliches und zweifelhaftes Gebilde, und die Ansicht des Aristoteles zeigt sich als die richtigere ".[72] Schopenhauer writes :

> . . . diese [vierte] Figur [ist] bloss die muthwillig auf den Kopf gestellte erste, keineswegs aber der Ausdruck eines wirklichen und der Vernunft näturlichen Gedankenganges . . .[73]

The same point of view is found in many later German writers, Christoph Sigwart [74] and Benno Erdmann [75] being among the more influential.

By the middle of the nineteenth century the spell of Kant began to weaken, and some German logicians took a more favorable view of the fourth figure. An outstanding example was Friederich Ueberweg, whose *System der Logik* includes a magisterial—but unaccountably neglected— analysis of the fourth figure, both historically and substantively.[76] A somewhat later work of this class is Theodor Ziehen's *Lehrbuch der Logik*.[77]

The English Hegelians followed the lead of their German confederates in recognizing the existence of the fourth figure but rejecting it as unnatural. Both Robert Latta [78] and Bernard Bosanquet [79] took this stand. [80]

---

[70] Hegel with characteristic incisiveness calls the fourth figure " a superfluous and even absurd addition of the Moderns to the three known to Aristotle." (W. Wallace, *The Logic of Hegel Translated from the Encyclopedia of the Philosophical Sciences* [Oxford, 1892], 2d ed., p. 321.) Hegel proposes an entirely different conception of syllogistic figures about which—like the proposed revision of his less eminent contemporary, Wilhelm Traugott Krug, whose *Logik* (§ 109) contains extensive criticisms of Lambert's ideas on the syllogistic figures—we shall here say nothing. (See Theodor Ziehen, *Lehrbuch der Logik* [*op. cit.*], p. 737.)

[71] See F. Ueberweg, *System der Logik* (*op. cit.*), p. 345.

[72] *Logische Untersuchungen*, (2 vols., Berlin, 1840), 3rd ed. 1870 (photoreprinted, Hildesheim, 1964), vol. I, p. 346 of the 3rd ed.

[73] *Die Welt als Wille und Vorstellung*, vol. II, bk. I, ch. 10.

[74] *Logik* (first published in Tübingen in 1873 ; *Logic*, tr. H. Dendy from the 2d ed., London, 1895). See p. 352 of the English version.

[75] *Logik* (2 vols., 2d ed., Halle a. S. 1907) ; see vol. I, sect. 522 : " Keine aus der Sache geschöpfte Betrachtung endlich, nur äusserlicher Schematismus, vermag der vierten Figur auszuhelfen."

[76] Bonn, 1857 ; 5th ed., 1882 ; see sect. 103.

[77] Bonn, 1920 ; see sect. 127.

[78] *The Elements of Logic* (London, 1895), revised ed. by A. Macbeth, (London, 1929), pp. 177 ff. of the revised ed.

[79] F. H. Bradley does not bother to attack the fourth figure of the syllogism—he is after bigger game, since for him the whole of syllogistic logic is a " chimaera." *The Principles of Logic* (2 vols., Oxford, 1883 ; 2d ed., 1922), vol. I, p. 248 and *passim*.

[80] *The Essentials of Logic* (London, 1895), p. 146.

In France the influence of the *Port Royal Logic* continued to be felt, with the result that the fourth figure tended to fare better than it did in Germany or England.[81]

Catholic logicians from Bossuet [82] to Maritain [83] almost invariably accept only the three Aristotelian figures and reject the fourth. They generally hold to the usual view of fourth figure syllogisms as indirect forms of first figure ones, as with the medievals.[84] Since, however, the differentiation between the major and minor terms is effected by them with respect to the conclusion, so that a fourth figure is unavoidable, a certain tension comes about in modern Thomist logic that was lacking in the medievals : the extra syllogisms are accepted as correct (valid) in one breath and disparaged as unnatural in the next.[85]

With the rise of symbolic logic, the fourth figure has viewed more or less standardly as being on the same plane as the second and third (apart from neo-Hegelian/idealist remnants, and outside the neo-Thomistic orbit). One outstanding early representative of this tendency is Louis Couturat.[86] Among the mass of writers of this tradition the place of the fourth figure is now so firm that even in a major treatise the opposition to it is dealt with only in an historical footnote.[87]

3. Critical Examination of Objections to the Fourth Figure

We have seen that the history of opposition to the fourth syllogistic figure began in antiquity. And we find that it extends down to the present day, when so able a logician as A. N. Prior writes that : "The

[81] See for example E. Rabier, *Logique* (Paris, 1886), ch. V.

[82] See A. Gratry, *Logic* (Engl. tr. by H. and M. Singer ; La Salle, Illinois, 1947), p. 306.

[83] Jacques Maritain, *An Introduction to Logic* (tr. I. Choquette, New York, 1939), see pp. 186–187.

[84] A. Gratry, *Logic* (*op. cit.*), pp. 271, 306–307. Compare the treatment of syllogistic figures in Joseph Gredt, *Elementa philosophiae Aristotelica-Thomisticae* (Rome, 1899 ; numerous reprints).

[85] Thus, for example, the 1950 logic-text, *Formal Logic*, of the influential Louvain Professor Joseph Dopp (tr. J. R. E. Ramirez and R. D. Sweeney ; New York, 1960) : "As for the indirect moods of the first figure (the 4th figure), they have hardly any proper role at all, and moreover do not seem very natural" (p. 163).

[86] "Précis de Logique Classique" = Appendice I to *La logique de Leibniz* (Paris, 1901). Couturat flatly says that the valid fourth-figure syllogisms "appartiennent à une figure spéciale, aussi légitime et aussi indépendente que les autres" (p. 455). But contrast C. S. Peirce who slights the fourth figure and wants to revive the indirect moods of Theophrastus. (*Collected Papers*, ed. C. Hartshorne and P. Weiss, vols. I/II [2d printing, Cambridge, Mass., 1960], §§ 2. 479–2. 506 ; cf. 1. 369.)

[87] For example, J. Jørgensen, *A Treatise of Formal Logic* (3 vols., Copenhagen and London, 1931) ; see vol. II, pp. 25–26, notes.

first three figures are in any case much more important than the fourth ".[88]

It is necessary to take brief notice—now from a purely logical rather than historical point of view—of the objections made against syllogistic reasoning in " the so-called fourth figure ".[89] We shall not here be dealing with conceptions of " syllogistic figure " which do not admit of a fourth figure at all, but rather with the views of those who, starting from a concept of *figure* that renders the fourth figure theoretically possible, seek to disparage the syllogisms of this figure as inferior or even illegitimate.

As best I can determine them, the objections to the fourth figure come to seven points.

Objection No. 1

Fourth figure syllogisms do not naturally occur in ordinary discourse, or—as many writers put it—they do not exhibit a " natural movement of thought ".[90] Thus we are told :

> It is evident then that, although the fourth figure is a *grammatical* figure it is not a distinct *logical* figure : in that which concerns *thought* the grammatical predicate of the conclusion is in reality its *subject*. For this reason every true logician must reject the fourth figure and consider it only as the indirect first.[91]

Reply to Objection No. 1

Some writers attempt to counter this point by giving concrete examples of reasonings which fit perfectly naturally into the fourth figure. Thus J. N. Keynes gives the example : " None of the Apostles were Greeks, Some Greeks are worthy of all honour, therefore, Some worthy of all honour are not Apostles ".[92] Some defenders of the fourth

---

[88] *Formal Logic* (Oxford, 1955), p. 111.

[89] C. Sigwart, *Logic*, 2d ed., tr. H. Dendy (2 vols., London, 1895), vol. I, p. 352.

[90] For a discussion sympathetic to this line of thought see for example, J. N. Keynes, *Studies and Exercises in Formal Logic* (6th ed., London, 1906), pp. 328–329. For a further elaboration of the reasons why the fourth figure is " seldom or never used " see W. H. Karslake, *Aids to the Study of Logic* (2 vols., Oxford, 1851), vol. I, pp. 74–77. Karslake borrows this expression, as well as most of his points, from Archbishop Richard Whately's *Logic* (bk. II, ch. iii, sect. 4). Whately lived 1787–1863, and published his *Logic* in London in 1825 (9th ed., 1848).

[91] Jacques Maritain, *An Introduction to Logic* (tr. I. Choquette, New York, 1937), p. 187, notes. This view is by no means peculiar to Catholic authorities. Compare, e.g., W. S. Jevons, *Elementary Lessons in Logic* (American ed., New York, 1920), pp. 147–148.

[92] J. N. Keynes, *Studies and Exercises in Formal Logic* (*op. cit.*), p. 329.

figure use a kind of *tu quoque* argument against other syllogisms. Thus L. Couturat writes :

> On allègue encore, contre les modes de la 4e figure, qu'ils ne sont pas *naturels*, qu'ils ont quelque chose contourné et de forcé. Mais ils ne sont pas plus " baroques " que *Baroco* ou *Bocardo*, et la plupart le sont moins.[93]

William Kneale rightly objects to this entire approach : " Sometimes they [critics of the fourth figure] talk as though the question at issue were about the way men naturally argue. If this is the problem, the proper way to solve it is to hold a large-scale empirical inquiry, but we must then contemplate the possibility that the fourth figure exists for some people and not for others ".[94] A *tour de force* here is a classic move by W. E. Johnson :

> An antiquated prejudice has long existed against the inclusion of the fourth figure in logical doctrine, and in support of this view the ground that has been most frequently urged is as follows :
>
> Any argument worthy of logical recognition must be such as would occur in ordinary discourse. Now it will be found that no argument occurring in ordinary discourse is in the fourth figure. Hence, no argument in the fourth figure is worthy of logical recognition.
>
> This argument, being in the fourth figure, refutes itself ; and therefore needs to be no further discussed.[95]

Objection No. 2

" What is called the fourth figure is only the first with a converted conclusion " and so " we do not actually reason in the fourth, but only in the first, and then if the occasion requires, convert the conclusion to the fourth ".[96]

Reply to Objection No. 2

The objection rests on : (1) the standard thesis that the first figure is the most " natural and perfect ", and (2) the contention that fourth-figure syllogisms reduce at once to the first figure by merely converting the conclusion (and/or transposing the premisses). We shall waive point (1). But (2) is clearly incorrect : " This account of figure 4

---

[93] *La logique de Leibniz* (Paris, 1901), pp. 455–456.

[94] W. and M. Kneale, *The Development of Logic* (Oxford, 1962), p. 101.

[95] W. E. Johnson, *Logic*, Part II (Cambridge, 1922), pp. 88–89.

[96] Francis Bowen, *Logic* (10th ed., Cambridge, Mass., 1874), p. 192. This is the position of innumerable textbooks. One of the more interesting examples of the older type is Asa Mahan, *The Science of Logic* (New York, 1857), pp. 132–133. The point was popularized by Kant, who in his essay on " Die falsche Spitzfindigkeit der vier syllogistischen Figuren erwiesen " (1762) held that only the first figure is natural and perfect ; the rest are artificial, and derive their validity only by conversion to the first figure.

cannot . . . be accepted since it does not apply to *Fesapo* or *Fresison*. For example, from the premisses of *Fesapo* (*No P is M* and *All M is S*) no conclusion whatever is obtainable in figure 1 ".[97]

The objection does, however, embody the grain of truth that the first-figure reduction of fourth-figure syllogisms requires only conversions (see Objection No. 4 below), and never calls for *per impossibile* reasoning (as is the case with *Baroco* in figure 2 and *Bocardo* in figure 3). But this shows at best that figure 4 is in some sense " less independent " of the first figure than is the case with figures 2 and 3 ; it clearly does not establish the dispensability (let alone illegitimacy) of the fourth figure.

There are writers such as H. W. B. Joseph who want to contend that a valid fourth-figure syllogism does not represent reasoning in a distinct figure because of " the fact that without one of these methods of validation [viz. reduction to the first figure] its conclusiveness is not apparent " and " is lacking something to be obvious ".[98] This view falls into the same dubious psychologism to be met with in Objection 1. Furthermore it is difficult to see how this sort of reductionism can be held to apply to the fourth figure but not to the second and third.[99] To carry this line of thought to its natural terminus we would have to reject (with Wolff and Kant) not only the fourth figure, but the second and third as well.

Objection No. 3

One (distinctly contra-traditionary) shortcoming was laid at the door of the fourth figure by Leibniz. Only the fourth figure, he remarked, cannot be derived from the first by *reductio* alone, but requires the—according to him logically less natural—process of conversion " so that it is farther removed by one degree than the second and third, which are on a level and equally removed from the first ".[100]

Reply to Objection No. 3

Historically, the objection flies in the face of the entire Aristotelian tradition, which from start to finish regards *per impossibile* argumentation

[97] J. N. Keynes, *Studies and Exercises in Formal Logic* (4th ed., London, 1906), p. 383. Compare P. Henle, " On the Fourth Figure of the Syllogism," *Philosophy of Science*, vol. 16 (1945), pp. 94–104.

[98] H. W. B. Joseph, *An Introduction to Logic* (2d ed., Oxford, 1916), p. 326.

[99] H. W. B. Joseph struggles manfully—but I think ineffectually—with this issue (*loc. cit.*)

[100] *New Essays Concerning Human Understanding*, bk. IV, ch. ii, sect. 1.

as a less desirable mode of syllogistic first-figure reduction than conversion. From the logical standpoint, the objection does not seem to have great force even on its own ground, since a *per impossibile* justification of the process of conversion itself is, of course, possible.

Objection No. 4

The reduction of the valid moods of the fourth figure by *per impossibil* reasoning does not lead outside the figure itself (unlike the three other figures).

Reply to Objection No. 4

This remark [101] is perfectly correct. But it does no more than to mark an item of difference between the fourth figure and the other three—and there are, of course, many others. It is unclear (to say the least) how this difference would amount to a point of inferiority.

The objection suggests the question : Could we take the valid moods of the fourth figure as axiomatic (instead of those of the first, as with Aristotle) and reduce the valid moods of the other figures to them by conversion and *reductio* ? This will be dealt with in Objection No. 7.

Objection No. 5

In the fourth figure neither term appears in the conclusion in the role it serves in the premises (i.e., the conclusion's subject is the predicate of its premiss and the conclusion's predicate is the subject of its premiss). We thus have a figure " with its premises looking one way, and its conclusion another ".[102]

Reply to Objection No. 5

The factual point is perfectly correct, but surely does not provide a cogent basis upon which to establish the inferiority of the fourth figure. In the piece of arithmetical reasoning

$$2 = a$$
$$\underline{4 = b}$$
$$a + b = 6$$

---

[101] Urged, so far as I know, only in W. and M. Kneale, *The Development of Logic* (*op. cit.*), p. 101.

[102] H. Karslake, *Aids to the Study of Logic* (*op. cit.*), vol. I, pp. 74–75. Compare J. Welton, *A Manual of Logic* (2 vols., 2d ed., London, 1896), vol. I, p. 314. This virtually standard objection goes back to Averroes. See C. Prantl, *Geschichte der Logik im Abendlande* (2 vols., Leipzig, 1855 ; photoreprinted Graz, 1955), vol. I, p. 571, and vol. II, pp. 389–390.

neither *a* nor *b* " occurs in the conclusion in the way in which it occurs in its premiss "—i.e., within the right-hand terminus of an identity— but this observation is patently irrelevant to whatever constitutes the merits of the reasoning in any logically germane sense.

Objection No. 6

" In calling the predicate of the conclusion in a syllogism the *major* term, then, Aristotle chose a name which was appropriate. . . . By the name *major* he wishes to indicate that the predicate is the more comprehensive term. . . . The *middle* term takes its name not simply from being a point of connexion between the other two, but from being really intermediate in comprehensiveness. This it is, however, only in the first figure. It is only there that the middle term is predicated of the minor, and the major predicated of it. In the second, it is predicate in each premiss ; in the third, the subject, of which both major and minor terms are predicated. But that which in the first figure is really a *middle* term between the major and minor serves equally in the others to be the means of establishing that relation between the major and minor which we prove ; and the nomenclature that is fixed by the first figure is extended to them all.

" It follows that Galen was wrong in assigning to a fourth and separate figure syllogisms in whose conclusion the most comprehensive term is subject, and the least comprehensive predicate. . . . The distinction of major and minor between terms is primarily that of greater and less comprehensiveness, and this is not altered by making the more comprehensive the subject, and the less the predicate, in the conclusion. But the fourth figure has been taught for so many centuries among the ' moods and figures ' of the syllogism, that for the sake of the history of Logic we cannot altogether ignore it, even while we recognize the error in which it had its birth ".[103]

Reply to Objection No. 6

We are dealing here with the most common objection to the fourth syllogistic figure : that on strictly Aristotelian grounds the figures of the syllogism are to be distinguished with respect to the extension or

[103] H. W. B. Joseph, *An Introduction to Logic* (2d ed., Oxford, 1916), pp. 261–262. Exactly the same account of the matter appears in such more recent books as M. R. Cohen and E. Nagel, *An Introduction to Logic and Scientific Method* (New York, 1932), p. 82 ; and J. A. Oesterle, *Logic* (2d ed., Englewood Cliffs, N.J., 1963), p. 177.

inclusiveness of the terms. " The theory of the syllogism has been much darkened by this addition [of a fourth figure]. For in erecting these arguments into a separate figure it is implied that the distinction between the major and minor term depends merely on their position in the conclusion, and is in no way intrinsic to the terms themselves ".[104] The strictly historical component of the thesis—that Aristotle's own distinction between the figures is based on term-inclusiveness relations—is highly disputable, but does not concern us here.[105] From the logical standpoint the view cannot be taken seriously. For, according to it, the two syllogisms

All cats are felines	All cats are felines
No dogs are felines	No felines are dogs
No dogs are cats	No dogs are cats

must be assigned to the same figure, since the extension relations among their terms are precisely the same. On the other hand the syllogisms

All Frenchmen are Europeans	All Frenchmen are Europeans
Some Frenchmen are physicians	Some Frenchman are Parisians
Some physicians are Europeans	Some Parisians are Europeans

would have to be assigned to different figures, since the extension relations among their terms are different. To justify a three-fold division of the syllogistic figures on this basis of term-extension relations is to introduce material considerations into the theory of the syllogism to a point that compromises its claims to be a branch of formal logic.

Some writers are apparently prepared to accept this consequence. Thus, after exhibiting the valid fourth figure syllogisms, C. Sigwart writes :

> It is evident that anyone forcing the concepts into this unnatural position must have forgotten all the fundamental presuppositions of the Aristotelian theory [viz. " recognizing the necessity of conceptual relations to be at the root of all inference "] ; the need of supplementing the Aristotelian doctrine [by the fourth figure] could only have been felt in a treatment which dealt with the external form alone.[106]

---

[104] H. W. B. Joseph, *An Introduction to Logic* (*op. cit.*), p. 259.
[105] I. M. Bochenski asserts flatly that Aristotle did so distinguish the figures : *Ancient Formal Logic* (Amsterdam, 1951), pp. 45–46. The actual complexity of the matter is discussed with exemplary precision in ch. IV of G. Patzig, *Die Aristotelische Syllogistik* (Abhandlungen der Akademie der Wissenschaften in Göttingen, philologisch-historische Klasse, dritte Folge, no. 42, 1959).
[106] C. Sigwart, *Logic*, vol. I (*op. cit.*), p. 352.

And compare H. W. B. Joseph :

It must always be remembered that the character of an argument is determined not by the form into which it is thrown in words, but by that which it assumes in our thought. This is our justification for recognizing the figures as distinct types. In particular cases, a syllogism may not belong to the figure into which it has been verbally compelled ; in others, it may be possible with the same terms to construct syllogisms in more than one figure ; but then there must be a real movement of thought in the process of conversion by which the change is effected. The theory of syllogism ought not to be regarded as a lesson in the manipulation of symbols and the application of the formulae. What we have to look to is the character of the thinking involved in it. . . .[107]

Here we complete the unhappy descent : we have moved from formal logic to material logic to psychologistic logic. It is one of the ironies of the history of logic that this degradation of syllogistic theory came to be defended in the name of faithfulness to the teachings of the great Stagirite.

Objection No. 7

If one takes the valid moods of the fourth figure as axiomatic, then one cannot derive all the valid syllogisms in all of the figures by the classical machinery of *reductio* and conversion. (Specifically one cannot derive AAA-1, *Barbara*.) But in the case of the three other figures, such a derivation is always possible.

Reply to Objection No. 7

The objection at issue seems to me to be the only one that possesses genuine force : it does establish the logical " inferiority " of the fourth figure in a plausible sense. It is yet another of the ironies of the history of logic that this (to our mind solitarily appropriate) ground for maintaining the inferiority of the fourth syllogistic figure is of our own devising and is nowhere to be found in the ramified literature of the subject, despite the innumerable discussions aimed at showing the inferiority of the fourth figure.

* * *

Our examination of objections to the fourth figure has one principal result : Given the now usual conception of " figure ", a fourth figure is inevitable. Not only is its *existence* thus beyond question, but its provision of valid syllogisms follows inexorably from the usual principles

[107] H. W. B. Joseph, *An Introduction to Logic* (*op. cit.*), pp. 330–331.

of syllogistic logic. There is no tenable basis for disparaging fourth figure reasonings, although it could reasonably be argued that from the *systematic* standpoint the fourth figure plays a somewhat less central or fundamental role than the others.[108]

[108] Here see our Objection No. 7, and cf. also the discussion in Storrs McCall, *Aristotle's Modal Syllogisms* (Amsterdam, 1963), pp. 28–29. Defenders of the fourth figure who want to put it on exactly the same logical plane as the second and third (such as L. Couturat in *La logique de Leibniz* [Paris, 1901 ; see especially pp. 455–456] have perhaps overstepped the mark of accuracy by some slight hair's breadth, though infinitely less so than the great phalanx of enemies to the figure. It is, more-over, undoubtedly the case that there are other systematic considerations—of perhaps a kind that seems artificial from the traditional approach to syllogistic logic—which militate favourably on behalf of the fourth figure. See, for example, D. D. Merrill, " Reduction to the Fourth Figure," *Mind*, vol. 74 (1965), pp. 66–70.

Chapter III

INTRODUCTION TO IBN AL-ṢALĀḤ'S TREATISE "ON THE FOURTH FIGURE OF THE CATEGORICAL SYLLOGISM"

Abū 'l-Futūḥ Aḥmad ibn Muhammad ibn al-Surā Najm al-Dīn ibn al-Ṣalāḥ was born in Persia around 1090. He flourished in Baghdad, where he became an influential physician, and died in Damascus in 1153.[1] Ibn al-Ṣalāḥ wrote primarily on scientific subjects (mathematics and astronomy). If his treatise with which we shall be concerned here is at all indicative, Ibn al-Ṣalāḥ's writings—none of which have yet been edited and studied—should prove of substantial interest, for he appears here as a highly competent scholar with an unusually keen interest in the historico-bibliographical side of his subject.

In 1936 the German Arabist Max Krause published a report on Islamic mathematical manuscripts he had examined in Istanbul during the winter of 1933–34.[2] He described a manuscript collection of treatises (rasā'il) by Ibn al-Ṣalāḥ in the possession of the Aya Sofya library in Istanbul,[3] which contains [4] (the uniquely extant copy of) the treatise "On the Fourth Figure of the Assertoric Figures [of the Syllogism] Attributed to Galen" (Maqālah fī 'l-shakl al-rābiʿ min ashkāl al-ḥaml wa-huwa 'l-mansūb ilā Jālīnūs). The presentation of the Arabic text of this treatise on the basis of the Aya Sofya version,[5] and its translation into English, will be the work of the two following chapters.

---

[1] See C. Brockelmann, Geschichte der Arabischen Litteratur, vol. I (2d ed., Leiden, 1943), p. 621, entry (4c) ; Supplement, vol. I (Leiden, 1937), p. 857 ; H. Suter, Die Mathematiker und Astronomen der Araber und ihre Werke (Leipzig, 1900), p. 120, entry 287 ; N. Rescher, The Development of Arabic Logic (Pittsburgh, 1964), pp. 173–174.

[2] "Stambuler Handschriften islamischer Mathematiker," Quellen und Studien zur Geschichte der Mathematik, Astronomie, und Physik, Abteilung B—Studien, vol. 3 (1936), pp. 437–532.

[3] Aya Sofya codex 4830.

[4] Folios 122b–128b.

[5] For a description of the manuscript codex see Krause's article (op. cit.).

Ibn al-Ṣalāḥ's treatise on the fourth syllogistic figure opens with a bibliographical introduction, whose principal contents we have already summarized. It is of great importance for the historian of logic because it contains information about the contents of significant works that are no longer extant. Moreover this treatise—which must antedate the work of Averroes by at least some thirty or forty years—represents a prior attribution of the fourth figure to Galen, the second prior such attribution yet found in an Arabic source (the first being that of Avicenna's *Al-Shifā'*). Because of its bibliographical detail, Ibn al-Ṣalāḥ's report is by far the most important of these attributions.

We learn at the close of this historico-bibliographical passage that in writing his own treatise on the fourth figure Ibn al-Ṣalāḥ had before him and was apparently influenced by another treatise (in an Arabic translation from the Syriac ?) on " The Fourth Figure of Galen " by " Dinḥā the Priest " (*D-nḥā al-qass*). There can be little doubt that this scholar is the Nestorian priest Denḥā (fl. ca. 800)—pupil of the important scholar and Nestorian catholicus Ishō bar Nūn (d. 828)—who in addition to his religious-theological writings is known to have written on logic.[6] (Dinḥā was certainly not a good logician, for—as Ibn al-Ṣalāḥ himself points out—he committed some elementary mistakes, including that of holding O-propositions to be convertible.) Ibn al-Ṣalāḥ further informs us that in the time of al-Kindī (d. ca. 870) a Syriac translation of a treatise of Galen's dealing with the fourth syllogistic figure was in circulation.

After its most valuable historical introduction, Ibn al-Ṣalāḥ's treatise is largely a routine—though more than ordinarily comprehensive and competent—analysis of the valid and invalid moods of the fourth figure. Its most surprising feature is the unusually favorable view it takes of this figure. For Ibn al-Ṣalāḥ maintains that the fourth figure is second only to the first in " perfection ", and is superior to the second and third. So far as our present information extends, this view is absolutely unique in the history of Arabic logic, and indeed almost unique in the entire history of logic down to the present century.[7]

---

[6] Anton Baumstark, *Geschichte der syrischen Literatur* (Bonn, 1922), p. 220.

[7] One other logician whom I know to hold this view is Peter Tartaret (fl. ca. 1480), who did much to gain acceptance for the fourth figure in modern European logic. He wrote : *Modi quartae figurae sunt evidentiores, quam modi secundae et tertiae, quia ad reducendum eos ad modos primae figurae paucioribus indigent, quam modi secundae vel tertiae, quia solum indigent transpositione praemissarum.* (C. Prantl, *Geschichte der Logik im Abendlande*, vol. IV [Leipzig, 1870 ; photoreprinted, Graz, 1955], p. 205, n. 162.) But Peter's position is tenable only because he views the fourth figure as the first with interchanged premisses.

The remaining two chapters of the present work will be devoted to Ibn al-Ṣalāḥ's treatise. Chapter V presents a transcription of the Aya Sofya manuscript. The transcription is generally " unimproved ", presenting the manuscript as Cromwell wished to be painted, " with the warts on", its imperfections showing through. Some key words and phrases are written with red ink in the manuscript, and these have been indicated in boldface print. In Chapter IV we present an English translation of the text. This translation is very literal—as must be the case if a rendition of a text of this sort is to answer to scholarly purposes. We have placed parentheses () around explanatory *elaborations* of the existing text, brackets [] around explanatory *additions* to the existing text, and double brackets [[]] around a conjectural rendition of an illegible portion of the manuscript. The division into sections and into paragraphs is, in most instances, without manuscript warrant and is indicated by the sense of the discussion alone. Even the division into sentences is, as any Arabist knows, in some measure arbitrary. To facilitate reference and cross-reference, the correlation of the translation with the text is indicated, the transition from line to line being shown by a vertical line |. For grammatical reasons this division cannot but be occasionally imperfect.

CHAPTER IV

ABŪ 'L-FUTŪḤ AḤMAD IBN MUḤAMMAD IBN AL-SURĀ IBN AL-ṢALĀḤ

TREATISE ON THE FOURTH FIGURE
OF THE FIGURES OF THE CATEGORICAL SYLLOGISM

122b1   In the Name of God, the Compassionate, the Merciful
                       By God's Help

2   The treatise of the shaikh Abū 'l-Futūḥ Aḥmad ibn Muḥammad
ibn al-Surā [ibn al-Ṣalāḥ], may God bless him, on the fourth figure

3 of | the figures of the assertoric [i.e., categorical] syllogism, which is
the figure attributed to Galen.

He said :

*   *   *

4 | We have found that most logicians discard this figure and reject
discussion (or : *mention*) of it, to the extent that we find the great

5 books (i.e., Great Commentaries) | which were written in commen-
tary upon *Prior Analytics* wholly devoid of its mention, with rare

6 exception among them. | These [exceptional treatises], even though
they may mention it in passing, some of them discard it, on the
grounds that it is removed from nature (i.e., is unnatural). Such is

7 found | in the great book which Abū ʿAlī ibn Sīnā compiled entitled

8 the *Kitāb al-shifāʾ*, in the fourth section (*faṣl*) | of the first chapter of
the " Book of the Syllogism " (*Kitāb al-qiyās*).[1] And some of them

9 reject it wholly and say that the division [of the figures] | does not
require it ; as is found, for example, in the commentary of Abū
'l-Faraj ibn al-Ṭayyib on the *Prior Analytics (Kitāb al-qiyās*).[2] He

---

[1] See pp. 9–10 of our Introduction.
[2] See N. Rescher, *The Development of Arabic Logic* (Pittsburgh, 1964), pp.
155–157.

10 criticizes Galen | and charges him with error without mentioning any proof at all for this, but simply by stating that Galen, though
11 outstanding | in medical matters, is not sound in logical matters.

Aḥmad ibn al-Ṭayyib al-Sarakhsī [3] has related in his epitome
12 | of the *Analytica [Priora]* that someone (literally : *a man*) mentioned to his teacher Yaʿqūb ibn Isḥāq al-Kindī [4] that he had a Syriac
13 treatise (*maqālah*) | of Galen on this topic (literally : *in this meaning*). But al-Kindī disavowed this [figure], and stated that a rational
14 division requires only three | figures and no others, and he has not acknowledged a fourth figure. And it has been related that Abū
15 Naṣr al-Fārābī [5] has a discussion (*kalām*) about the standing of | this figure and its illegitimacy (literally : *its rejection*), which I have not seen.

These, then, are the books which we have seen that have afforded
16 discussion (or : *mention*) of this | figure.

As for the rest of the books and commentaries which have come
17 down to us, those of Aristotle and Alexander and Porphyry | and other ancients and moderns, we do not find them affording discussion (or : *mention*) of it, but all of them when they divide the figures
18 | divide them into three, and stipulate that they have no fourth. And we have found Galen [himself] doing likewise in the ninth
19 chapter (*maqālah*) | of the *Peri Apodeixeōs*, for he divided the assertoric (or : *categorical*) figures into three only and concluded with the
20 statement that they have no fourth ; | and he does likewise in his *Book on the Enumeration of Syllogisms*. [But] we have not yet seen from among the books on logic [attributed to Galen] despite the great
21 | number of which the *Fihrist* [6] speaks, any except for these two books. [But] there happened to come to us the discourse (*maqālah*)
22 by a man | known as Dinḥā the Priest (*D-nḥā al-qass*) [7] entitled " The Fourth Figure of Galen ". When we examined it we found it
23 defective | in meaning with respect to the conditions (i.e., validity-conditions) of the figure, [and] about the enumeration of its kinds

[3] See *ibid.*, p. 109. This man was the star pupil of the shortly-to-be-mentioned al-Kindī.

[4] On al-Kindī as a logician see *ibid.*, pp. 100–103.

[5] See *ibid.*, pp. 122–128.

[6] That is, the famous book of Ibn al-Nadīm (d. ca. 995) for whose role as a source of information on the history of logic see *ibid.*, pp. 136–137.

[7] Although he draws (possibly heavily) on the treatise of this obscure Syriac Christian scholar—for whom see Chapter II above—Ibn al-Ṣalāḥ takes an independent attitude towards his statements, and does not hesitate to disagree with him flatly (and rightly) at 128a7–128b4.

(or : *moods*), and in (the fact that) it makes some of its sterile (i.e.,
123a1 invalid) (moods) valid, and in its poor [8] understanding of | the first
figure to which this (fourth) figure is reduced. When we perceived
2 this, we investigated this figure and its conditions | for validity and
its similarities with the three well-known figures and [also] its
differences from them—I mean the differentia (or : *divisions*) which
3 divide | it from them. And [we made] an enumeration of its moods,
one by one, and a display of the demonstration of their validity or
4 a proof of their invalidity, and the grounds for this. | Now is the
time to begin with this.

*   *   *

Thus we say that the middle term must be either : (1) predicate
5 in one of the | two premisses [of a syllogism] and subject in the other ;
and if this is so, then it (the middle term) must be either (*a*) predicate
6 in the minor | and subject in the major, and this is what is called the
7 first figure ; or (*b*) subject in the minor | and predicate in the major,
and this is the fourth additional figure, which in my opinion should
8 be put second in the ordering, | as I shall discuss in what is to follow.
Or (2) the middle term is subject in each of the two premisses, and
9 this is the second figure, | but with this [i.e., our own] division [of the
figures] it is necessary that it be the third. Or (3) it is subject in both
of them (viz. the premisses) and this is the third [figure] according to
10 the old division, | and the fourth according to our view.
11   If an opponent opposes us and says : The statement " that | the
middle term is predicate in one of the two premisses and subject in
12 the other " is already introduced in the first figure | and this fourth
figure is extra (i.e., superfluous) ; [then] we say to this opponent :
By my life, two [very distinct] divisions enter into it, seeing that the
13 first figure is not | the one whose middle term is predicate in one of
14 the two premisses and subject in the other without restriction, | but
each one of the two premisses is specifically-identified.[9] Thus the one
(division) whose two premisses are specifically-identified becomes
15 like a species for the one whose premisses are | unrestricted. If we
were to take the two premisses as unrestricted, then it would be

---

[8] Reading *r-d-'-'-h* for the *r-d-'-h* of the manuscript.
[9] Note that Ibn al-Ṣalāḥ is perfectly clear that two distinct conceptions of
figure (i.e., our Conceptions No. 2 and 4 in section 9 of Chapter I) are at issue.
Accepting the former as correct, he does not attribute the latter either to
Aristotle or to al-Fārābī, but only to an anonymous " opponent."

correct for us to say with respect to the first figure that it is one of its
16 [validity] conditions | that the major be universal and the minor affirmative, because in this fourth, additional figure we do not need
17 this condition, and | it [viz. the fourth figure] is [also] included under the [arguments] whose two premises are unrestricted.[10]

Suppose someone set up a division of the simple bodies into two
18 species, into | the heavy (or : *gravitational*) and the celestial, and shows this by saying that a motion is either linear or rotational,
19 | and so if it is rotational, then it is celestial, and if it is linear then
20 it is heavy, because the heavy moves towards the center | in a straight line. Then we say in answer to this that if you say that the
21 heavy is that which moves in a straight line | purely and simply, without specifying this as a motion towards the center, then it would
22 be true for you to say that there are two [simple] bodies. | But when you specified this [motion] as a motion *towards* the center, there arises out of the division a third type [of motion], namely motion *from*
23 | the center. And so the simple bodies would be three and not two : the celestial and the heavy and the light, even though the light
123b1 | and the heavy are two species of linear motion, which is divided from the celestial.[11]

2 So also we say about the moods | of the figures with regard to their quantity that they are four : this is because either (1) both the two
3 premises are universal, or | (2) [both are] particular, or (3) the major is universal and the minor particular, or (4) the minor is
4 universal | and the major particular. It would not be permissible for
5 us to say that these four moods are [only] three, | because the division requires this when we take them in this way : either both
6 premises are universal, or | [both] particular or one of the two is universal and the other particular. Consequently, we accept this statement of the matter absolutely (or : *unqualifiedly*).

*   *   *

7 So we start | upon an enumeration of the moods to determine those of them which are conclusion-yielding (i.e., valid), and we

---

[10] The point is that if the premises were not distinguished, thus separating fourth-figure syllogisms from those of the first figure, the indicated validity-condition would not apply to the (unexpurgated) first figure.

[11] For fuller discussion of the set of ideas at issue here, see N. Rescher and H. Khatchadourian, " Al-Kindī's Treatise on the Distinctiveness of the Celestial Sphere," *Islamic Studies*, vol. 4 (1965), pp. 46-54.

ignore the rest because it is included in a genus one of whose two
8 species we have already determined. | It is this [enumeration] which
differentiates this figure from the three [other] figures in regard to
9 the syllogism. As for [the way] in which | it is different in its validity
conditions from their conditions [for validity], it will become evident
through an exposition of the things which are common to the four
10 figures | and those in which they differ.

We say that the four figures have [certain] conditions [for validity]
11 common to all, whereby they do not yield-a-conclusion | when
present in any one of the four [moods]. [Furthermore] they are
differentiated by conditions which are specific to each one of them.
12 Thus [the conditions] | in which the four [figures] share is (1) that
there is no syllogism from two negatives [as premisess], (2) nor from
two particulars, and (3) not if the minor is negative and the major
13 | particular.¹²

As for what differentiates them, it is that the first [figure] requires
14 that the minor be affirmative and the major universal. | And this
additional figure (i.e., the fourth) requires that one premiss be
15 affirmative and the other universal—I mean that | one of the two
may not be negative particular. And its (the fourth figure's) second
[special] condition is that there not be an assembling of a particular
16 affirmative minor | and a universal affirmative major.¹³

By these two conditions the three figures become differentiated ¹⁴
[from the fourth] in [terms of] the conditions that govern them :
17 (I) As for the difference in [terms of] the first condition | in rela-
tion to the first figure, this is evident. This is so because even if it
[viz. the fourth figure] shares with it [the first] [the fact] that one
18 of its premisses not be | negative particular, just as in the first figure,
it nevertheless differs from it in that in this [first] figure it must be
19 specified which one of the two is the affirmative one | among the two
premisses, namely the minor, and which of the two is the universal
one, namely the major.¹⁵

For this [fourth] figure we have accepted [in addition to its own
20 specific validity-conditions] | two absolute (i.e., general) and non-
differentiating conditions [for validity] : (1) the first is that one of

---

¹² It is perhaps unnecessary to observe that these rules are correct.
¹³ The special condition for figures two and three are not dealt with until
126a16 ff. below.
¹⁴ Reading *b-'-y-n* for *b-'-n.*
¹⁵ Note that this specification was not made for the fourth figure at lines
14–15 above, and need not be made.

the two [premises] be affirmative—either one of them, be it the
21 minor or the major—and (2) the other | [is that one of the two
premises be] universal, either one of them also.[16] And on the basis
(literally : *from here*) it (i.e., the fourth figure) yields-a-conclusion
from a universal affirmative minor and a particular affirmative
22 major,[17] | which is contrary to what is [the case] in the first figure, in
which this connection does not yield-a-conclusion (i.e., is invalid).[18]
23 And by this [first] condition | it (i.e., the fourth figure) is differen-
tiated from two other figures. For the second figure [has a valid
124a1 syllogism such that] the minor is particular negative,[19] i.e., | the
fourth of its [valid] moods ; and the third figure [has a valid
syllogism such that] the major is particular negative,[20] to wit the
2 sixth | of its [valid] moods.[21]

(II) As for the second condition which we have set-as-a-condition
for this additional figure (i.e., the fourth figure),[22] it is that there not
3 be | in it a union between a particular affirmative minor and a
universal affirmative major. This differentiates it [from] the first
4 figure | and the third ; [23] and makes it share [something in common]
with the second [figure], because the second requires this, because its
5 condition is that its two premises be opposites | in quality.

(III) As for the third difference between this [fourth] figure and
6 the rest, this | regards its conclusion, and it is this : The first figure
yields four desired conclusions—I mean the affirmative universal and
7 the negative | universal and the affirmative particular and the nega-
tive particular. And the second [figure] yields two desired con-
8 clusions, namely a negative universal and a negative | particular,
because it does not yield an affirmative at all. And the third figure
yields two desired conclusions, namely an affirmative particular and
9 a negative | particular, and it does not yield a universal at all. But
this [fourth] figure yields three desired conclusions : a negative
universal and a negative particular and an affirmative particular.
10 | Thus this [fourth figure] is distinct (or : *differentiated*) from the first

---

[16] This was already stated at lines 12–13 above.
[17] This was already stated at lines 15–16 above.
[18] That is, *IA*. The point is that the fourth figure has a valid syllogism of the
mood *IAX* (namely *IAI-4, Dimaris*), whereas the first figure does not.
[19] Namely *AOO-2, Baroko*.
[20] Namely *OAO-3, Bokardo*.
[21] See below, 125b20.
[22] Cf. 123b15–16.
[23] Both of which have valid syllogisms of the *AIX* form, namely *Darii* and
Datisi.

figure in that the first yields an affirmative universal [conclusion],
11 and this figure does not yield it at all. | And it is distinct from the
second, because the second does not yield an affirmative [conclusion]
at all, and this figure does yield an affirmative particular. And it is
12 distinct from the third figure | because the third figure does not yield
a universal [conclusion] at all, and this figure can yield a negative
universal.

13 (IV) As for the fourth difference | between this [fourth] figure and
the other figures, it obtains with regard to the number of [valid]
14 moods. For the number of moods of this | figure which are conclu-
sion-yielding (i.e., valid) is five, but is four in the first [figure], and
in the second four, and in the third six.

*   *   *

15 As for | [the fact] that this [fourth] figure has to be put after the
first [and so given priority over the orthodox second and third
figures], this is shown in two ways.

(I) The first of the two is that it [viz. the fourth figure] is of the
16 [same] division | as the first—I mean that it shares [with the first
figure] in that the middle term is subject in one of the two premises
17 and predicate | in the other. But it [i.e., the first figure] is superior to
it [i.e., the fourth figure] in that it is nearer to nature (i.e., is more
natural). It [i.e., the first figure] does not need to be demonstrated
18 [i.e., is self-evident], but this [fourth figure] cannot dispense | with
a demonstration. Thus the first takes precedence over it in this
19 way with a precedence that is necessary to it. | And the second
[i.e., the fourth figure] follows after it [i.e., the first] as being a
species of [the same] division, because judgment in this figure and
20 the first are judged to be two species of the same division. | And the
two other figures are judged together with these two, judged [to be]
two [further] species of [one and the same] division of the [same]
genus of the first and the fourth, additional [figure].[24] The species is

24 The discussion here seems to envisage the following classification-schemes.

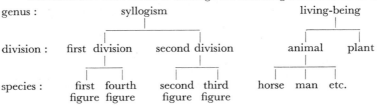

58

21 closer | to [the other species of] the [same] division than to [another]
a division of its genus. An example of this is that *man* is nearer to
horse which is within [the same] division [of the genus *living-being*,

22 viz. the division *animal*] | than to *plant* which is [another] division of
its genus, I mean [the genus of] *animal* [viz. the genus *living-being*].

23 This then is one of two ways for the sake of which | this figure is put
second to the first.

(II) The second way in which this [fourth] additional figure is

124b1 superior to the other two figures (viz. no.'s two and three) | is in the
number of desired conclusions [validly yielded by it]. This is so
because it (i.e., the fourth figure) yields three desired conclusions—

2 I mean a negative universal and an affirmative | particular and
a negative particular. [But] these other two figures yield only two
desired conclusions—I mean that the second yields only a negative

3 universal | and a negative particular, and the third yields an affirma-
tive particular and a negative particular. And just as the philosopher

4 [i.e., Aristotle] gave precedence to the first figure | over these other
two figures because of its yielding [all] four desired conclusions, so

5 likewise you must follow him in | giving priority to this figure over
the others, because it yields three desired conclusions, since it

6 assembles in its conclusions the [entire] assemblage | of the con-
clusions of these other two figures.[25]

* * *

Suppose it is said that this figure must be put after the other two

7 figures | because it is further from nature (i.e., more unnatural),
because it requires for [the validation of] some of its moods a con-

8 version, i.e., conversion of both the two premises | whereas these
[other] two figures do not require conversion of both the two
premises.

Then we say : Its requiring two conversions [for reduction to the

9 first figure] | does not make it necessary to put this figure after these
two (i.e., the second and third), because in both of these figures there

10 is also a requirement for a conversion, I mean a conversion | of one
of the two premises or a conversion of the conclusion, as [is the case]

11 in the second mood of the second figure, i.e., the mood | whose
minor is converted—I mean the one composed of a universal
affirmative major and a univeral negative minor, which requires

---

[25] The second figure has E and O conclusions, the third I and O, and the
fourth has all three forms : E, I, and O.

12 | a conversion of the conclusion.[26] And similarly, the third figure—
since it requires in one of its moods conversion of the major, namely

13 in the fourth mood | whose major is universal affirmative and whose
minor is particular affirmative—[also] requires conversion of the
conclusion.[27]

14 | These two figures—I mean the second and the third—are more
remote [in the scale of priority] from the additional (i.e., the fourth)

15 figure by something specific to them, this being that | each one of the
two of them contains a mood whose validity cannot be proved
[sc. by reduction to the first figure] except by a *reductio ad absurdum*.

16 Such is [the case] with the fourth mood of the second figure | which
is the one whose major is universal affirmative and whose minor is
particular negative.[28] And such is [also] [the case] with the sixth

17 mood | of the third figure, whose minor is universal affirmative and
whose major is particular negative.[29] But there is not among the

18 moods | of this additional [fourth] figure any which requires proof
by a *reductio*, but all of them can be proved by conversion. It is well

19 known that demonstration | by *reductio ad absurdum* is more remote
and distant from nature (i.e., is more unnatural) than demonstration
by conversion.

20 Suppose it is said that this [fourth] figure requires | for [reduction
of] some of its moods [as many as] three conversions—I mean conversion of each one of its two premisses and [also] its conclusion, and

21 that [consequently] from this standpoint | [[it is inferior]].[30] We say
[in reply] that there is not among the [valid] moods of this figure any

22 which requires three conversions at all, as will be shown in | [[the
sequel. Some]] [31] of its moods, namely the third and the fifth, do not
require conversion of the conclusion.[32] And when the conclusion is

---

[26] *AEE-2 (Camestres)* is reduced by conversion of the conclusion *and the minor*
premiss to *EAE-1 (Celarent)*.

[27] *AII-3 (Datisi)* is reduced by conversion of the minor premiss [not the conclusion!!] to *AII-1 (Darii)*.

[28] *AOO-2 (Baroko)* cannot be reduced to a first figure syllogism by conversion.
But if we conjoin the major premiss with the contradictory of the conclusion,
we obtain the contradictory of the minor premiss by an *AAA-1 (Barbara)*
syllogism.

[29] *OAO-3 (Bokardo)* cannot be reduced to a first figure syllogism by conversion.
But if we conjoin the minor premiss with the contradictory of the conclusion
we obtain the contradictory of the major premiss by an *AAA-1 (Barbara)*
syllogism.

[30] The text is illegible here, but the sense is clear.

[31] The text is illegible here, but the sense is again clear.

[32] The moods in question are *EAO-4 (Fesapo)* and *EIO-4 (Fresison)*. For
details see below.

23 converted, conversion | of [either] one of the two premisses is not
required at all, let alone both of them, because conversion of the
125a1 conclusion interchanges | the ordering of the two premisses.[33] When
they (the premisses) are interchanged in this figure—I mean when
we put each of the two [premisses] in place of the other—we do not
2 not require | any conversion of the two premisses, which is contrary
to what is [the situation] in the second figure and the third. The
3 two moods in which there is an interchange | in the ordering of the
premisses in these two figures [are reduced] by converting in both
of them [also] one of the two premisses.[34]

*   *   *

4   Suppose it is said that this [fourth] figure | is rendered dispensable
by the first figure. We say : The two other figures are [also]
rendered dispensable by the first on account of what has been shown
5 | in the *Book of Prior Analytics*. If dispensability necessitates annul-
ment, then these two figures should [also] be annulled. However,
6 | this [result] is not readily admissable. But we must classify and
enumerate and discuss fully the divisions in every matter, whenever
7 possible. | This then is what it is necessary for us to say about this
matter from this standpoint.

*   *   *

Thus let us now discuss the conditions (sc. validity-conditions)
8 | of this [fourth] figure.

We say that this figure has [certain] conditions in common
9 with the other three figures. These are : (1) that | there is no [valid]
syllogism in these four figures by a conjunction in them of two
negatives, nor (2) of two particulars, nor (3) of a negative minor
10 | and a particular major.[35]

And [further] this [fourth] figure has in common with the first one
[special rather than general] condition—just as there is in common
11 between each one of these | other two figures and the first one single
condition. And the condition which is common to this [fourth] figure
12 and the first figure | is that one of the two premisses must not be

---

[33] Thus reducing the syllogism to the first figure by one single conversion.

[34] That is *AEE-2* (*Cesare*) reduces to *EAE-1* (*Celerent*) when its conclusion and
minor premiss are converted and the premisses interchanged, and *IAI-3*
(*Disamis*) reduces to *AII-1* (*Darii*) when its conclusion and major premiss are
converted and the premisses interchanged.

[35] Compare above, 123b11–13.

61

13 negative particular. This very condition is necessitated in | the first
figure by our making it a condition that the minor be affirmative
14 and the major universal. [But] as for the two other figures, | there
is in each of the two of them [a valid syllogism with] a premiss which
is negative particular.[36]
15 As for the condition which is common to | each of these other two
figures and the first, we [find that] they are as follows : The major
16 of the second figure must necessarily | be universal, just as this was
made a condition for the major of the first figure. The minor of the
17 third figure must be affirmative, | just as this was made a condition
for the minor of the first figure. And just as there is a condition for the
18 first figure which is common to both its premisses—namely | that
neither of the two be negative particular—likewise this is [a con-
dition] common to the two premisses of the additional [fourth]
figure. And just as there is a condition which is a special-charac-
19 teristic | of the major [premiss] [in the first figure]—namely that it be
universal—likewise this is a special-characteristic for the major of
the second [figure]. And just as there is a condition which is a
20 special-characteristic of the minor [in the first figure]— | namely
that it be affirmative—likewise this is a special-characteristic for the
minor of the third figure.
As for the condition which is a special-characteristic of this
21 | [fourth] additional figure, it is that there not be assembled in its
unions [37] whose minor is particular [38] and whose major is affirmative
22 universal, | just as there is a special-condition for the second figure
which is a special-characteristic of it but not the three remaining
23 figures, namely that the premisses be opposed | in quality.
As for the third figure, it is [39] specially-characterized by [only]
one single condition. This is so since if it is said regarding it that it
125b1 has two conditions, | one of these two being (1) that its minor be
affirmative, and the other condition being (2) that there must be in it
2 a universal premiss, [we reply that] this [second] is not | special-
characteristics for it [i.e., the third figure].[40] For the last-named

---

[36] AOO-2 (Baroko) in the second figure and OAO-3 (Bokardo) in the third.

[37] We here render by " unite " and its cognates the techical terms of Arabic
logic based on the root z-w-j, and by " assemble " and its cognates those based
on j-m-ʻ.

[38] The text reads " affirmative universal," which makes the statement
incorrect.

[39] The MS reads " it is not." I would suppose fa-huwa in place of fa-lam.

[40] The first of these conditions is a (needed) validity-condition for the third
figure.

condition does not specially characterize it, but is contained in what
3 is common to [all] the four figures, | namely that there is no [valid] syllogism in [any of] them [composed] of two particulars [as premisses].[41]

And for this [reason]—I mean that there is but one condition for the third figure [over and above the general conditions for all four
4 of the figures]— | its conclusion-yielding (i.e., valid) moods are numerous, and become six, in contrast to the rest of the remaining
5 figures, for their [valid] moods are less | than this.

*   *   *

For as to the reason why there are in the first [figure] four valid
6 moods, and in the second [figure] also four moods, and in | the third [figure] six moods, and in the [fourth] additional figure five moods, this is something we shall now show to follow necessarily from these
7 | conditions. This is so because the number of unions in each one of the figures is, according to what [proper] division necessitates,
8 | [a total of] sixteen unions—I mean unions whose premisses are
9 delimited by quantity-indicators.[42] For if we brought in | the quantitatively-indefinite propositions into the total, then there would be thirty-six unions.[43] However—since a quantitatively indefinite proposition has exactly the same force as a particular,
10 | because it is indefinite that it is universal and indefinite that it is particular, and so whether it obtains universally is open to doubt but
11 that it obtains | particularly is certain, in as much as that which is true if the whole is [necessarily] true of the part—we put the particular in place of the indefinite.
12 | And this shows [also] that the division required for the quantitatively definite [syllogisms] [leads to] sixteen unions, as follows :
13 | The two premisses cannot fail to be both universal or both particu-
14 lar, or to be a universal and a particular, | or a particular and a universal. These are the four " unions ". And each one of these
15 unions cannot fail to be | of four types, namely that both [premisses]

[41] The first-named condition—viz. that the minor be affirmative—does hold for the third figure (and also for the first).

[42] That is, contain " all " or " some " like " Some men are physicians " but unlike the quantitatively indefinite " Men are physicians."

[43] If we added the quantitatively indefinite affirmative and negative proposition to the four categoricals, A, E, I, and O, then the two premisses would generate not $4 \times 4 = 16$ but $6 \times 6 = 36$ combinations.

are together negatives or are together affirmatives, or are an affirma-
16 tive and a negative, | or a negative and an affirmative. Thus, when
17 these other four types multiply by four the first [four] types, | these
sixteen unions arise from this.

Of these, four are universals, namely these : (1) two universal
18 affirmatives, | (2) two universal negatives, (3) a universal affirmative
[major] and a universal negative [minor], (4) a universal negative
[major] and a universal affirmative [minor].[44]

19 | And four others are particulars, coming with the first [four] to
20 eight. They are these : (5) two particular affirmatives, | (6) two
particular negatives, (7) a particular affirmative [minor] and a
particular negative [major], (8) a particular negative [minor] and
a particular affirmative [major].

21 | And four others [composed] of a universal minor and a particular
22 major come with the preceding to twelve. They are these : | (9) a
universal affirmative [minor] and a particular affirmative [major],
(10) a universal negative [minor] and a particular negative [major],
23 (11) a universal affirmative [minor] | and a particular negative
[major], (12) a universal negative [minor] and a particular affirmative [major].

126a1   And four other connections,[45] composed | of two premisses whose
minor is particular and whose major is universal, come with the
2 totality of the preceding unions to | [a total of] sixteen unions. They
are these : (13) a particular affirmative [minor] and a universal
3 affirmative [major], (14) a particular negative [minor] | and a
universal negative [major], (15) a particular affirmative [minor] and
a universal negative [major], (16) a particular negative [minor]
and a universal affirmative [major].[46]

*   *   *

[44] Note that the usual minor-major ordering is reversed here. (This becomes
apparent at 127a2-9 below.) This leads to confusion and error at some points,
e.g. at 126a14 below.
[45] We translate by " connect " and its cognates the technical terms based on
the root *q-r-n*.
[46] Thus the 16 " unions " are as follows (note we follow the modern Western
practice of putting the major—rather than as in the standard Arabic usage the
minor—first) :

1. AA	5. II	9. IA	13. AI
2. EE	6. OO	10. OE	14. EO
3. AE	7. OI	11. OA	15. EI
4. EA	8. IO	12. IE	16. AO

The conception of such sixteen types of syllogistic mood (*modus*) along these

4   These | sixteen unions are such that eight of them are invalidated
by the three [general] conditions [of validity] that condition the
5 totality of the four figures. | This is so because of three conditions,
namely that there is no [valid] syllogism [composed] of two particu-
6 lars nor of two negatives | nor of a negative minor and a particular
major.[47]

   By the first condition—namely that there is no syllogism [com-
7 posed] of two particulars— | four unions are invalidated, namely the
fifth and the sixth and the seventh and the eighth. And by the
8 condition that | there is no syllogism [composed] of two negatives,
three [further] connections are invalidated, namely the second and
9 the tenth and the fourteenth. And by the condition | that there is no
syllogism [composed] of a negative minor and a particular major one
10 of the remaining unions is invalidated, namely the twelfth. | Thus
the unions that are invalid can be in all of the figures by way
11 of the general [conditions] come to a total of eight, | as has been
discussed.

   (I) The two special validity-conditions which have been set in
12 in the first figure render ineffective four further unions. | By the
condition for it (viz. the first figure) that the minor be affirmative
two of the remaining unions are rendered ineffective, namely the
13 third and the sixth. | And by the condition for it that the major
be universal two of the remaining six unions are rendered ineffective,
14 | namely the ninth and the eleventh. Thus there remain four valid
15 unions in the first figure, namely | the first, the fourth,[48] the thir-
teenth, and the fifteenth.[49]

   (II) In just the same way also, by the two [special] conditions for
16 the second figure | there remain in it of the eight remaining connec-
17 tions [only] four valid moods. This is so because | one of its two
conditions is the same as one of the two conditions of the first [figure],

<hr>

lines, with undifferentiated premises, as a basis for the enumeration of
syllogisms and the analysis of their validity goes back at least to Appuleius,
whose Latin term for these "unions" is *coniugationes*. See C. Prantl, *Geschichte
der Logik im Abendlande*, vol. I (*op. cit.*), pp. 587–591. Bochenski (*Formal Logic*
[*op. cit.*], p. 219) suggests that Albertus Magnus borrowed this combinatorial
procedure from the Arabs, but—while he may well have done so—it could have
been taken from a Latin source, if not Appuleius then perhaps Boethius. Its
ultimate origin is certainly Greek, and probably Stoic (cf. Prantl's biting
remark, *op. cit.*, p. 591).

[47] See above, 123b11–13.

[48] The text reads "third" but this is wrong in the light of line 12 above. On
the source of the confusion see our note at 125b18.

[49] Namely *AA, EA, AI*, and *EI*; i.e., *Barbara, Celarent, Darii*, and *Ferio*.

namely that its major be universal. Thereby there is rendered

18 ineffective | in it (the second figure) the two connections remaining in the first [figure] through this condition (i.e., after it has been imposed), namely the ninth and the eleventh.[50] As for the second

19 condition | which specially-characterizes it (viz. the second figure)— namely that its two premisses be opposite in quality—two more of

20 the remaining six unions are rendered ineffective by it, | namely the first and the thirteenth. There thus remain to it (viz. the second

21 figure) four valid unions, namely the third and the fourth | and the fifteenth and the sixteenth.[51]

(III) Similarly there are six valid connections in the third figure

22 among the eight | that remain, because one condition which specially-

23 characterizes it is [also] one | condition of the first [figure], I mean [the condition] that the minor be affirmative.[52] Two connections are rendered ineffective by it, namely the third and the sixteenth,

126b1 | which are [also] the two which are eliminated in the first figure by this condition.[53] There remain six valid moods, as we have said,

2 namely | the first and the fourth and the ninth and the eleventh, and the thirteenth and the fifteenth.[54]

3 | (IV) Three of the eight remaining connections are rendered ineffective by the two conditions we have set for the [fourth]

4 additional figure. This is [as follows] : | One of these two conditions is that it is not feasible that one of the two premisses be negative

5 particular.[55] | By this [condition] two connections are rendered ineffective, namely the eleventh and the sixteenth. These two unions

6 are rendered ineffective | in the first [figure] by a combination of its two conditions, because by each of the two conditions of the first

7 [figure] one of the two is rendered ineffective.[56] | And by the other condition—namely that there is no [valid] syllogism in this [figure] [composed] of a particular affirmative minor and a universal

8 affirmative major— | one [further] mood is rendered invalid, namely the thirteenth. Thus there remain five valid moods [in the fourth

---

[50] Cf. above, 126a13–14.
[51] Namely *AE*, *EA*, *EI*, and *AO* ; i.e., *Camestres, Cesare, Festino, Baroko.*
[52] Compare above, 125a23–125b3.
[53] Cf. above, 126a12.
[54] Namely *AA*, *EA*, *IA*, *OA*, *AI*, and *EI* ; i.e., *Darapti, Felapton, Disamis, Bokardo, Datisi,* and *Ferison.*
[55] Cf. 125a12 above.
[56] The 16th union, *AO*, is ruled out by the first condition (that the minor be affirmative), and the 11th union, *OA*, is ruled out by the second condition (that the major be universal). Cf. above, 126a12–14.

9 figure], namely the first and the third | and the fourth and the ninth and the fifteenth.[57]

We have already mentioned that the total number of [valid]
10 unions in all | of the four figures is nineteen. The entire collection
11 of them comes to 64 | unions, of which 45 are invalid and 19 are valid moods.

*   *   *

It remains among the things for which we took responsibility above
12 | to give a demonstration regarding the five moods which we have stated to be valid in the [fourth] additional figure and to show the
13 truth of this, and likewise | to show that the eleven remaining moods are invalid. And now is the time to begin with this by an enumeration of unions.

14 | **The first mood** [consisting] of two universal affirmatives yields
15 an affirmative particular.[58] For example : *Every A is B* | and *Every C is A*, so I say that it yields *Some B is C*. The demonstration of this is that if we change the ordering [of the premises] in that we make
16 | the major the minor and the minor the major, then [the syllogism] comes to be as follows : *Every C is A* and *Every A is B* yields *Every C*
17 *is B*, by the first mood | of the first figure. This conclusion converts and becomes *Some B is C* which is what we desired. An example of
18 this | from current usage is : *Every rational creature is an animal* and *Every man is a rational creature*, so this yields *Some animal is a man*.

19 **The second [mood]** | [consists] of two universal negatives. It is invalid because it yields an affirmative universal and a negative
20 universal together. Whatever is of this kind | will be invalid, because it does not yield any single thing but the opposite (or : *contrary*) thing [also]. Thus there is no syllogism [here], because a syllogism—
21 according to what Aristotle defined— | is " a discourse (or : *statement*) composed of two statements which necessitate by their nature one
22 [other] thing by necessity ".[59] | But this [pair of premises now at issue] does not necessitate any one thing. In this way Aristotle
23 showed invalid connections [to be such] | in the *Book of Prior Analytics*. An example of this which yields an affirmative universal is : *No*

---

[57] Namely *AA, AE, EA, IA,* and *EI* ; i.e., *Bramantip, Camenes, Fesapo, Dimaris,* and *Fresison.*

[58] Here we have *AAI*-4 (*Bramantip*).

[59] *Anal. Pr.,* I, 1 ; 24b18–20. If we supposed a previous reading of *ka-dhālika* in place of *li-dhātihā,* this would substitute " from their being so " for " by their nature ", bringing the definition closer to the Greek original.

67

127a1 *single rock is a man* | and *No single animal is a rock*, so *Every man is an*
animal. And an example which yields a negative universal is : *No single*

2 *stone is a man* | and *No single horse is a stone*, so *No single man is a horse*.[60]

3   **The third [mood]**, the second valid mood [of this figure], | [con-
sisting] of two universals, the major one being affirmative and the
minor one negative, yields a negative universal [conclusion].[61] For

4 example : *No A is B* | and *Every C is A* yields *No B is C*. When we
change the ordering [of the premises] by making the minor the

5 major | and the major the minor, it becomes as follows : *Every C is A*

6 and *No A is B* yields *No C is B* by the second mood | of the first
figure.[62] We convert this conclusion so that it becomes *No B is C*,

7 which is | what we desired. An example from current usage is : *No*
single animal is a stone and *Every man is an animal*, so this yields *No single*

8 *stone* | *is a man.*

    The fourth [mood] is the third of the valid moods [in this figure].

9 [It consists] of two universals, the major one being negative | and the
minor one affirmative and yields a negative particular [conclusion].[63]

10 For example : *Every A is B* and *No C is A* yields *Not every* | *B is C*
[that is, *Some B is not C*]. This is so [because] when we convert both
of the two premises it (i.e., the syllogism) becomes as follows, *Some*

11 *B is A*—because the affirmative universal | converts to a particular
affirmative—and *No A is C*, because a negative universal converts
like the original itself [i.e., converts to another negative universal],

12 and so this yields *Not* | *every B is C*, by the fourth mood of the first
figure.[64] An example of this from current usage is : *Every man is an*

13 *animal* and *No single horse* | *is a man*, so *Not every animal is a horse* [that is,
Some animal is not a horse].

14   **The fifth mood** [consists] of two particular affirmatives. | It is
invalid because it yields an affirmative universal and a negative
universal, as we shall discuss generally [below] regarding these four

15 connections | which [consist] of two particulars.[65]

    [60] This example makes clear the method of invalidity demonstration at issue.
To exhibit that a certain form of premises does not lead to any valid syllogism
we present a pair of substitution-instances such that : (1) the two conclusions
represent contrary (or contradictory) forms, and (2) the pair of premises and
the conclusion is true in each case. When this is possible, it is clearly established
that no syllogistic conclusion can validly be drawn from the premises.
    [61] Here we have *AEE*-4 (*Camenes*).
    [62] That is by *EAE*-1 (*Celarent*).
    [63] Here we have *EAO*-4 (*Fesapo*).
    [64] That is by *EIO*-1 (*Ferio*).
    [65] See the discussion of the eighth mood below where the four cases numbered
5–8 are dealt with generally.

The sixth mood [consists] of two particular negatives. It is also
16 invalid, | yielding two opposites (or : *contraries*).

The seventh mood [consists] of a particular affirmative minor
17 and a particular | negative major. It is also invalid, yielding two
opposites (or : *contraries*) together.

18 **The eighth mood** consists of a particular | negative minor and
a particular affirmative major. It is invalid. The terms which yield
19 an affirmative universal [conclusion] | in these four unions are
" man " and " animal " and " body "— in that if we take " animal "
20 as the shared (i.e., middle) term | and " man " as the minor term
and " body " as the major. As for the terms which yield a negative
21 universal [conclusion], | they are " white " and " man " and
" bird " in that we take " white " as the shared (i.e., middle) term
22 and " man " | as the minor and " bird " as the major.

23 **The ninth mood,** the fourth of the valid moods, | [consisting] of
a universal affirmative minor and a particular affirmative major,
127b1 yields an affirmative particular [conclusion].[66] For example : | *Every
A is B* and *Some C is A*, then I say that this yields *Some B is C.* The
2 demonstration of this is that we take each | of the two premises in
place of its companion so that it [i.e., the minor] becomes thus :
3 *Some C is A* and *Every A is B*— | [then] this yields *Some C is B* by the
second mood of the first figure ;[67] and by conversion of this con-
4 clusion it becomes | *Some B is C.* This is what we wanted. An example
from current usage is : *Every man is an animal* and *Some rational
5 creature | is a man*, so *Some man is a rational creature.*

The tenth mood [consists] of a universal negative minor and a
6 particular | negative major. It is invalid. It yields two opposites (or :
contraries) together. An example of how it yields an affirmative
7 universal is : *No single man | is a horse* and *Not every sleeping creature is
a man* (that is, *Some sleeping creature is not a man*) so *Every horse is
a sleeping creature.* And an example which yields a negative universal
8 [conclusion] is : *No single man | is a stone* and *Not every sleeping creature
is a man* (that is, *Some sleeping creature is not a man*), so *No single stone is
a sleeping creature.*

9 **The eleventh mood** | consists of a universal affirmative minor
and a particular negative major. It is invalid. It yields two
10 opposites (or : *contraries*). An example which | yields an affirmative
universal is : *Every man is an animal* and *Not every corporeal thing is*

---

[66] Here we have *IAI-4 (Dimaris)*.
[67] That is, by *AII-1 (Darii)*.

a man (that is, *Some corporeal thing is not a man*) so *Every animal is*

11 *a corporeal thing.* And an example | which yields a negative universal is : *Every animal is a sensible creature* and *Not every stone is an animal* (that is, *Some stone is not an animal*) so *No single sensible creature is a stone.*

12 | We ought not to hasten to the opinion that we imagined in this example that we stated [68] a negative universal when we stated, *Not*

13 | *every stone is an animal,* and that [instead] we should have said, *No single stone is an animal.* [If] this [last statement] [is true], the state-

14 ment | *Not every stone is an animal* is true also, because the negative particular is true along with the negative universal [but not conversely].

15 We have | followed the precedent of Aristotle in this example, this

16 being so because he does similarly in a place in the *Book* | *of Prior Analytics,* in that [part] of it [which treats] of connections that are [composed] of a negative particular minor and an affirmative

17 universal major | in the first figure, when he wishes to show that this is not valid. He speaks in this very way in the source [viz. in *Prior*

18 *Analytics*] : [69] For example | if A is present in all B, and B is not

19 present in some C or is not present in all C | —terms for this being " living " [70] and " man " and " white "—then the taking [71] from the " white " of something of which " man " cannot be predicated,

20 | as for example " swan " and " snow ", [leads to the result that] " living " can be predicated of all of the former [viz. " man "] but cannot be predicated of anything of the latter [viz. " swan " or

21 " snow "].[72] | In this way one makes " man " into the middle term in both of the two examples, [both] that which yields an

22 affirmative universal, | [[and that which yields a negative universal,

---

[68] The text reads " concluded."

[69] *Anal. Pr.*, I, 4 ; 26b1–9.

[70] The Arabic term used here can also fit the Greek for " animal " used in Aristotle's text.

[71] The Greek *ekthesis.*

[72] Lines 18–20 correspond to *Anal. Pr.* 26b3–8. The logic of the situation here is as follows. The initial premisses are :

| All B is A | All men are living |
| Some C is not B | Some white things are not men |

These premisses might conceivably be supposed to lead to some particular conclusion " Some C (is) (is not) A," that is, either " Some white things are not living," or " Some white things are living." But if this were so, then one of the trios

All B is A	All B is A
Some C is not B	Some C is not B
All C is A	No C is A

would have to be an inconsistent triad. That the first is not is shown by the case, A = living, B = man, C = swan, i.e.,

and " living " into]] the major term in both of the [i.e., these] two examples. As for the minor term, we make it in [the example] which
23 yields the affirmative | universal " swan ", and in the one which yields the negative universal " snow ". Then " living " [would, if the inference were valid, be predicated] of this [viz. snow] in an
128a1 affirmative universal. The connections are [then] as follows : | *Not every swan is a man* (that is, *Some swan is not a man*) and *Every man is an animal*, so this yields *Every swan is an animal*. It is well-known that the
2 statement *Not | every swan is a man* (that is, *Some swan is not a man*) does not provide that *Some swan is a man* because the negative
3 particular [must] be true together with the negative | universal. And they (i.e., the terms in question) are used similarly in the other example, which is the one that yields the negative universal [con-
4 clusion] *Not every snow is a man* | and *Every man is an animal*, so *No single snow is an animal*.[73]

5 **The twelfth mood** [consists] of a universal negative minor | and a particular affirmative major. It is invalid because it yields two opposites (or : *contraries*). An example which yields an affirmative
6 universal [conclusion] is : | *No man is a horse* and *Some sleeping creature is a man* which thus yields *Every horse is a sleeping creature*. And an
7 example which yields a negative universal [conclusion] is : | *No man is a stone* and *Some animal is a man* so *No stone is an animal*.

8 Dinḥā [74] has maintained that | this mood is valid. An example he gave [to show this] is, *No A is B* and *Some C is A*, and so he maintained
9 that this yields *Not every | B is C* (that is, *Some B is not C*).[75] If we change the ordering of this—putting each one of the two premises
10 in place of the other— | then it becomes as follows : *Some C is A* and *No A is B* yielding *Not [every] C is B* (that is, *Some C is not B*), by the
11 fourth [valid] mood of the first figure.[76] | However we [ourselves] hold that this is not valid, because the desired conclusion which this yields is *Not every B is C* (that is, *Some B is not C*) because the major

> All men are living beings
> Some swans are not men
> All swans are living beings
And that the second trio is no inconsistent triad is shown by the case, A = living, B = man, C = snow, i.e.,
> All men are living beings
> Some snows are not men
> No snows are living beings

[73] The text, in obvious error, reads " a man " instead of " an animal."
[74] On " Dinḥā the Priest " see our note at 122b22 above.
[75] That is, it was held that the *IEO*-4 syllogism is valid.
[76] That is, by an *EIO*-1 (*Ferio*) syllogism.

12 [term] | is C, and this conclusion is the converse of *Not [every] C is B* (that is, *Some C is not B*). But we cannot convert this conclusion

13 because it is negative particular. | Thus this result is the converse of the desired-conclusion and not the desired-conclusion [itself]. Thus if Dinḥā went so far [as to hold] that this mood is valid, then

14 we could put | into the first figure two other valid moods, namely : (1) the mood whose minor is negative universal and whose major is

15 universal | affirmative, and (2) the mood whose minor is universal negative and whose major is particular affirmative.[77] An example

16 of this is, *No | B is A* and *Every A is C* yields *Not every C is B* (that is,

17 *Some C is not B*), because if we convert both of two premisses | [and interchange them] the mood becomes as follows, namely : *Some C is A* and *No A is B*, so this yields *Not every C is B* (that is, *Some C is not B*)

18 by the fourth [valid] mood | of the first figure.[78] However, the desired [conclusion] is *Some B is [not] C*, and it (i.e., the particular

19 negative) does not convert. Therefore Aristotle did not hold | that these two moods are valid ; although some of the ancients made them both out to be valid. But the objection to it, as we have stated

20 | in denying this, is that they yield the converse of the desired [conclusion] and do not yield the desired conclusion [itself.]

21 **The thirteenth mood** [consists] of a particular | affirmative minor and a universal affirmative major. It is invalid because it yields two opposites (or : *contraries*) together. An example of this

22 with an affirmative | universal [conclusion] is : *Some animals are men* and *Every rational creature is an animal* and so *Every man is a rational creature*. And an example with a negative universal [conclusion] is :

23 *Some | animal is a man* and *Every horse is an animal* so *Not a single man is a horse.*

128b1 Dinḥā also has made this mood out | to be valid because he put both the two premisses in place of the other, and [held to be]

2 necessitated by the two of them an affirmative | particular.[79] [But] he did not know that if the minor is put in place of the major this

3 leads to a mood in the first figure | composed of an affirmative

---

[77] We know that *EIO*-1 is valid. Thus if the *O* conclusion converted, then *IEO*-1 would be valid (converting both the conclusion and the *E*-premiss *EIO*-1) and so *a fortiori AEO*-1 would be valid also.

[78] That is, by *EIO*-1 (*Ferio*).

[79] The logician at issue thus held that *AII*-4 syllogisms are valid, and also *IEO*-4 (as above). By contrast we learned from the report of al-Qazwīnī al-Kātibī (cited in section 4 of Chapter I) that certain " moderns " viewed *AOO*-4, *OAO*-4 and *IEO*-4 syllogisms as valid.

universal minor and an affirmative [particular] major.[80] But this is

4 invalid because it is one of the conditions of the first [figure] | that the major be universal. This is thought to be something well-known about the first figure.

5 **The fourteenth mood** | [consists] of a particular negative minor and a universal negative major. It is invalid because it yields two

6 opposites (or : *contraries*) together. An example of this | with an affirmative universal [conclusion] is : *Not every man is a neighing creature* (that is, *Some man is not a neighing creature*) and *No single horse is*

7 *a man* so *Every neighing creature is a horse*. And an example | with a negative universal [conclusion] is : *Not every animal is a man* (that is, *Some animal is not a man*) and *No single stone is an animal*, so *No single man is a stone.*

8 | **The fifteenth mood,** which is the fifth of the valid moods [in

9 the fourth figure] [consisting] of a particular affirmative | minor and a universal negative major, yields a negative particular [con-

10 clusion].[81] For example : *Some A is B* and *No C is A* yields | that consequently *Not every B is C* (that is, *Some B is not C*). When we convert both of the two premisses this becomes as follows : *Some B is A*

11 and *No A is C* | yields that consequently *Not every B is C* (that is, *Some B is not C*) by the fourth mood of the first figure.[82] An example

12 for current usage is : *Some animals are* | *white* and *No single stone is an animal*, so *Not everything white is a stone* (that is, *Some white thing is not a stone*).

13 **The sixteenth mood** | [consists] of a particular negative minor and a universal affirmative major. It is invalid. It yields two

14 opposites (or : *contraries*) together. An example of this | which yields an affirmative universal [conclusion] is : *Not every animal is a man* (that is, *Some animal is not a man*) and *Every rational creature is an animal*

15 and so *Every man is a rational creature*.[83] And one | which yields a negative universal is : *Not every animal is a man* and *Every horse is an animal*, so *Not a single man is a horse.*

16 | These then are the valid and the invalid moods [of the fourth figure].

*　　　*　　　*

---

[80] That is, it becomes necessary to uphold the validity of *IAI*-1, for that of *AII*-1 (*Darii*) will not serve.

[81] Here we have *EAO*-4 (*Fesapo*).

[82] That is by *EIO*-1 (*Ferio*).

[83] The text mistakenly reads " is an animal " instead of " is a rational creature."

[All that is needful] has now been shown, except that what we
17 have shown was only [done] taking | both the two premisses to be
absolute (assertoric). As for [what happens] if the two premisses are
18 both necessary | or both possible or mixtures of these three kinds—
I mean the absolute (assertoric) and the necessary and the possible—
19 | this requires another proof. Already the ancients separated this
20 branch of the science from | the first, and of this sort [also] is what
the moderns among the Alexandrians knew of the matter, in small
21 part. We shall deal separately | with such cases in a treatise following
this one, God the All-high willing.

*   *   *

22 | The treatise is completed. Praise be to God alone.

CHAPTER V

ابو الفتوح احمد بن محمد بن السرى بن الصلاح

* * *

مقاله

فى

الشكل الرابع

من اشكال القياس

[ايا صوفيا ٤٨٣٠]

بسم الله الرحمن الرحيم   استعنت بالله

2 مقاله للشيخ ابى الفتوح احمد بن محمد بن السرى رحمه الله فى الشكل الرابع من

3 اشكــــال القيــــاس الحملى وهو الشكـــل المنسوب الى جالينوس. قال

4 | انــا وجدنا جل المنطقيين يطرحون هذا الشكل ويبلغون ذكره حتى انا نجد الكتب

5 الكبار | التى دونت فى شرح انالوطيقا الاولى خاليه عن ذكره اصلا ما خلا

6 الشاذ منها فانها | وان ألمت بذكره فمنها ما تطرحه وتعلل ذلك بانه بعيد عن الطبع

7 مثل ما يوجد | فى الكتاب الاعظم الذى جمعه الرئيس ابو على بن سينا ووسمه

8 بكتاب الشفاء فى الفصل | الرابع من المقاله الاولى من كتاب القياس ومنها ما

9 ترده اصلا وتقول ان القسمــه | لا تقتضيه كما يوجد فى شرح ابى الفرج بن

10 الطيب بكتاب القياس فانه يثلب جالينوس | ويخطيه من غير دليل ذكره البته

11 فى ذلك بل بمجرد القول بان الجـالينوس وان كان مبرزا | فى الامور الطبية فلا

12 تسلم له الامور المنطقيه وقد حكى احمد بن الطيب السرخسى لاختصاره |

لانالوطيقا ان رجلا ذكر لاستاذه يعقوب بن اسحق الكندى ان عنده مقاله

13 سريانيه | لجـالينوس فى هنا المعنى فانكر ذلك الكندى وذكر ان قسمه العقل

14 لا تقتضى الا ثلثه | اشكال لا غير ولم يعترف بشكل رابع وقد حكى ان لابى

15 نصر الفرابى كلاما فى ترتيب | هذا الشكل ورده لم اشاهده فهذه الكتب التى

16 شاهدناها تعرضت لذكر هذا | الشكل فاما باقى الكتب والشروع التى انتهت

17 الينا لارسطوطاليس والاسكندر وفرفوريوس | وغيرهم من القدماء والحدث فلم

18 نجدهم تعرضوا لذكره بل كل منهم اذا قسم الاشكال | قسمها الى ثلثه ونص

19 على انها لا رابع لها وكذلك وجدنا جالينوس فعل فى المقاله التاسعه | من كتاب

البرهان فانه قسم الاشكال الحمليه الى ثلثه فقط وجزم القول بانه لا رابع لها

20 | وكذلك فعل فى كتابه فى احصاء القياسات ولم نكن شاهدنا من كتبه فى

21 المنطق على كثرتها | بحسب ما ينطق الفهرست بها الا هذين الكتابين وقد كانت

22 وقعت الينا مقاله لرجل | يعرف بدنحا القس موسومه بالشكل الرابع لجالينوس

23 فلما تأملناها وجدناها مختله | المعنى فى فيما يشترطه الشكل فى تعداد ضروبه وجعل

بعض العقم منتجه وفى رداه فهم || الشكل الاول الذى يرد اليه هذا الشكل

2 فلما رأينا ذلك بحثنا عن هذا الشكل وعن شرايطه | فى انتاجه ومشاركته لثلثه

3 الاشكال المعروفه ومخالفته لها اعنى الفصول التى ينفصل | بها عنها وتعداد ضروبه

4 ضربا ضربا واقامة البرهان على المنتج منها وبيان العقيم والنص عليه | وهذا حين

ابتدى بذلك **فنقول** ان الحد الاوسط لا يخلوا من ان يكون محمولا فى احدى

5 | المقدمتين وموضوعا فى الاخرى فاذا كان كذلك فلا يخلوا من ان يكون محمولا

6 فى الصغرى | وموضوعا فى الكبرى وهذا هو الذى يسمى الشكل الاول. او يكون

7 موضوعا فى الصغرى | ومحمولا فى الكبرى وهذا هو الشكل الرابع المزيد وعندى

8 انه ينبغى ان نجعل ثانيا فى الترتيب | لما ساذكره فيما بعد. او يكون الحد الاوسط

9 محمولا فى كلتى المقدمتين وهذا هو الشكل الثانى | ومع هذه القسمه ينبغى ان

10 يكون ثالثا او يكون موضوعا فيهما وهو الشكل الثالث على القسمه | القديمه وعلى

11 راينا فهو الرابع. فان اعترضت علينا معترض وقال ان بقولك ان | الحد الاوسط

محمول فى احدى المقدمتين وموضوع فى الاخرى قد دخل فيه الشكل الاول

12 | وهذا الشكل الرابع المزيد. قلنا لعمرى ان القسمين داخلان فيه لكن ليس

13 الشكل الاول | هو الذى يكون فيه الحد الاوسط محمولا فى احدى المقدمتين

14 وموضوعا فى الاخرى مطلقا | بل تتعين كل واحده من المقدمتين فيكون الذى

15 مقدمتاه معينتين كالنوع الذى مقدمتاه | مطلقتين ولو اخذنا المقدمتين مطلقتين

16 لما صح فى الشكل الاول ان نقول ان من شريطته | ان تكون كبراه كليه

17 وصغراه موجبه لان فى هذا الشكل الرابع المزيد لا نحتاج الى هذه الشريطه | وهو

داخل تحت المطلق المقدمتين ولو ان قاسما قسم الاجسام البسيطه الى نوعين الى

18 | ثقيل والى فلكى وبين ذلك بان يقال ان الحركه اما ان تكون مستقيمه او تكون

19 مستديره | فان كانت مستديره فهى الفلكيه وان كانت مستقيمه فهى الثقيل

20 لان الثقيل يتحرك الى الوسط | على خط مستقيم لقلنا له فى جراب ذلك لو انك

21 قلت ان الثقيل هو الذى يتحرك على خط | مستقيم مطلقا من غير ان تخصص

22 ذلك بالتحرك الى الوسط لصح لك ان الاجسام اثنان | ولكن لما خصصت ذلك

23 بالتحرك الى الوسط جاء من القسمه ضرب ثالث وهو المتحرك من | الوسط

فتكون الاجسام البسيطه ثلثه لا اثنان فلكى وخفيف وثقيل وان كان الخفيف

123b1 || والثقيل نوعين للمستقيم الحركه الذى هو قسم الفلكى كذلك ايضا نقول فى

2 ضروب | الاشكال من حيث الكميه انها اربعه وذلك انه اما ان تكون المقدمتان

3 كليتين واما | جزئيتين واما ان تكون الكبرى كليه والصغرى جزئيه واما ان

4 تكون الصغرى كليه | والكبرى جزئيه ولا يسوغ لنا ان نقول ان هذه الاربعه

5 الضروب هي ثلثه | لان القسمه تقتضى ذلك بان نأخذها هكذا. اما ان

6 تكون المقدمتان كليتين واما | جزئيتين او احداهما كليه والاخرى جزئيه فنأخذ

7 الكلام هاهنا مطلقا واذا شرعنا | فى تعداد الضروب بعين ما نحتاج اليه ونتغافل

8 عن الباقى لانه داخل تحت جنس قد بينا | احد نوعيه فهذا ما تباين به هذا

9 الشكل الثلثه الاشكال الاخر فى قياسيته. واما ما | تباين الاخر فى شرايط انتاجه

10 وشرايطها فتبين ببياننا ما تشترك فيه الاشكال | الاربعه وتباين. فنقول ان الاربعه

11 الاشكال تشترك فى شرايط تعمها | متى وجدت فى واحد من الاربعه

12 وتباين بشرايط تخص كل واحد منها فالذى تشترك | فيه الاربعه ان لا قياس عن

13 سالبتين ولا عن جزئيتين ولا اذا كانت الصغرى سالبه والكبرى | جزئيه واما ما

14 تتباين به فهو ان الاول يحتاج ان تكون صغراه موجبه وكبراه كليه | وهذا الشكل

15 المزيد يحتاج ان تكون احدى مقدمتيه موجبه والاخرى كليه اعنى انه | لا تكون

احداهما سالبه جزئيه والشريطه[1] الثانية له ان لا يجمع فيه بين صغرا جزئيه

16 موجبه | وكبرى كليه موجبه وبهاتين الشريطتين باين الثلثه الاشكال فى الشرايط

17 اما مباينه بالشريطه | الاولى للشكل الاول فظاهر وذلك لانه وان شاركه فى انه

18 لا تكون احدى مقدمتيه | سالبه جزئيه كما فى الشكل الاول ولكنه باينه فى ان

19 ذلك الشكل قد عين فيه ايما هو الموجب | من مقدمتيه وهى الصغرى[2] او ايما

20 هو الكلى وهو الكبرى وهذا الشكل قد اخذنا الشريطتين | مطلقتين غير معينتين

21 فان احداهما موجبه ايهما كانت الصغرى ام الكبرى والاخرى | كليه ايهما

كانت ايضا ومن هاهنا انتج عن صغرى كليه موجبه وكبرى جزئيه موجبه

22 بخلاف[3] | بخلاف ما كان فى الشكل الاول فان هذا الاقتران فيه لا ينتج وبهذه

23 الشريطه باين | الشكلين الاخرين ايضا فان الشكل الثانى قد تكون صغراه

124a1 جزئيه سالبه وهو الضرب || الرابع من ضروبه والشكل الثالث قد تكون كبراه

2 جزئيه سالبه كما فى الضرب السادس من | ضروبه فاما الشريطه الثانيه التى

3 اشترطناها فى هذا الشكل المزيد وهو ان لا يكون | فيه ازدواج بين جزئيه موجبه

4 صغرى وكليه موجبه كبرى فانه باين بهذا الشكل الاول | والثالث وشارك بها

5 الثانى لان الثانى يلزم فيه ذلك لان من شريطته ان تختلف | مقدمتاه فى الكيف

6 واما المباينه الثالثه بين هذا الشكل وبين الاشكال الباقيه فهو من | حيث نتائجه

---

¹ In the MS: الشر.   ² In the MS: الصغر.   ³ Thus in the MS.

وذلك ان الشكل الاول ينتج المطالب الاربعة اعنى الايجاب الكلى والسلب

7 | الكلى والايجـاب الجزىء والسلب الجزىء والشكل الثانى ينتج مطلبين وهما السلب

8 الكلى والسلب | الجزىء لانه لا ينتج ايجابا البته والشكل الثالث ينتج مطلبين هما

9 الايجاب الجزىء والسلب | الجزىء ولا ينتج كليا البته وهذا الشكل ينتج ثلثه

10 مطالب سلبا كليا وسلبا جزئيا وايجابا جزئيا | فهو مباين للشكل الاول من حيث ان

11 الاول ينتج ايجابا كليا وهذا الشكل لا ينتجه البته | ويباين الثانى لان الثانى لا

12 ينتج ايجابا البته وهذا الشكل قد ينتج ايجابا جزئيا ويباين الشكل | الثالث لان

الشكل الثالث لا ينتج كليا البته وهذا الشكل قد ينتج سالبا كليا واما المباينه

13 الرابعه | بين هذا الشكل والاشكال الاخر فهو من حيث عدد الضروب فـان

14 عدد ضروب هذا | الشكل المنتجه خمسه وهى فى الاول اربعه وفى الثانى اربعه

15 وفى الثالث سته. فاما | ان هذا الشكل ينبغى ان يجعل تاليا للاول فيبين من

16 وجهين احدهما انه قسيم الاول | فى القسمه اعنى انه شاركه فى ان حد الاوسط

17 موضوع فى احدى المقدمتين ومحمول | فى الاخرى ويفضل عليه بانه اقرب الى

18 الطبع ومستغنى فى البيان عنه وهذا | عنه يستغنى فلا وهذا فيقدم عليه الاول

19 من هذا الوجه يقدم ما هو ضرورى التقدم | وتلاه الثانى تلوا الانواع القسيمه

20 لان حكم هذا الشكل مع الاول حكم نوعين قسيمين | وحكم الشكلين الاخرين

21 معهما حكم نوعين قسيمين لجنس الاول والرابع المزيد والنوع اقرب | الى قسيمه

22 من قسم جنسه مثال ذلك ان الانسان اقرب الى الفرس الذى هو قسيمه | من

النبـات الذى هو قسيم جنسه اعنى الحيوان فهذا احد الوجهين الذى لاجله جعل

23 | هذا الشكل ثانيا للاول والوجه الثانى ان هذا الشكل المزيد يفضل على الشكلين

124b1 || الاخرين فى عدد المطالب المنتجه وذلك انه ينتج ثلثه مطالب اعنى سلبا كليا

2 وايجابا | جزويا وسلبا جزويا وذانك الشكلان لا ينتجان الا مطلبين اعنى الثانى لا

3 ينتج الا سلبا كليا | وسلبا جزويا والثالث ينتج ايجابا جزويا وسلبا جزويا وكما

4 ان الفيلسوف قدم الشكل | الاول على هذين الشكلين لانتاجه المطالب الاربعه

5 هكذا ينبغى ان يقتدى به فى | تقديم هذا الشكل عليهما لانتاجه ثلث مطالب

6 ولهذا ما اجتمع فى نتائجه مجموع | نتائج ذينك الشكلين الاخيرين فان قيل هذا

7 الشكل ينبغى ان يؤخر عن الشكلين الاخرين | لانه بعيد عن الطبع ولهذا ما

8 يحتاج بعض ضروبه الى عكس اعنى عكس كلتى المقدمتين | وليس فى ذينك

الشكلين ما يحتاج الى عكس كلتى المقدمتين فانا نقول كونه يحتاج الى عكسين

9 | لا يوجب له التأخر عنهما لأن فى ذينك الشكلين ما يحتاج الى عكسين ايضا

10 أعنى عكس | احدى المقدمتين وعكس النتيجه كما فى الضرب الثانى من الشكل

11 الثانى وهو الضرب الذى | بعكس صغراه اعنى المؤلف من كليه موجبه كبرى

12 وكليه سالبه صغرى فانه يحتاج الى | عكس النتيجه وكذلك الشكل الثالث اذا

13 ما احتيج فى احد ضروبه الى عكس الكبرى وهو الضرب | الرابع الذى كبراه

14 كليه موجبه وصغراه جزئيه موجبه فانه يحتاج الى عكس النتيجه | وقد زاد هذان

15 الشكلان اعنى الثانى والثالث فى البعد عن المزيد شىء خصاه وذلك ان | فى كل

واحد منهما ضرب لا يبين انتاجه الا بالخلف كما فى الضرب الرابع من الشكل

16 | الثانى وهو الذى كبراه كليه موجبه وصغراه جزئيه سالبه وكما فى الضرب

17 السادس | من الشكل الثالث الذى صغراه كليه موجبه وكبراه جزئيه سالبه وليس

18 فى ضروب | هذا الشكل المزيد ما يحتاج الى ان يبين بالخلف بل باجمعها تبين

19 بالعكس ولا خفا ان برهان | الخلف اغرب وابعد عن الطبع من برهان العكس

20 فان قيل بان هذا الشكل قد يحتاج فى | بعض ضروبه الى ثلث عكوس اعنى

21 عكس كل واحد من المقدمتين والنتيجه ومن هذه الجهه | (؟)(4) قلنا ليس فى

ضروب هذا الشكل ما يحتاج الى ثلثه عكوس البته على ما سيتبين فى |

22 (؟)(5) ضروبه وهما الثالث والخامس لا يحتاج الى عكس النتيجه ومتى عكست

23 النتيجه لم يحتج | عكس واحده من المقدمتين البته فضلا عن كلتيهما لانه انما

125a1 تعكس النتيجه عند تبديل || ترتيب المقدمتين ومتى تبدلتا فى هذا الشكل أعنى

2 ان نجعل احداهما فى موضع الاخرى لم نحتج | الى عكس شىء من المقدمات

3 بخلاف ما فى الشكل الثانى والثالث فان الضربين الذين تبدل فيهما | ترتيب

مقدمات هذين الشكلين تعكس فيهما احدى المقدمتين. فان قيل ان هذا الشكل

4 | قد استغنى عنه بالشكل الاول قلنا وقد استغنى عن الشكلين الاخرين بالاولى

5 بحسب ما تبين | فى كتاب انالوطيقا الاولى فان كان الاستغناء يوجب الالغا فيلغى

6 هذين الشكلين لكن | ذلك ليس بسايغ بل يجب علينا التصنيف والتعديد واستيفا

7 الاقسام فى كل امر مهما امكن | فهذا ما احتجنا ان نقوله فى هذا المعنى من هذا

8 الوجه. فلنذكر الان شرايط | هذا الشكل فنقول ان لهذا الشكل شرايط تعمه مع

---

4 Illegible word of 3-4 letters.   5 Illegible word of 3-4 letters.

9 الاشكال الاخر الثلثه وهو انه | لا قياس فى هذه الاشكال الاربعه باجمعها عن

10 سالبتين ولا عن جزئيتين ولا عن صغرى | سالبه وكبرا جزئيه ويعم هذا الشكل

11 والاول شريطه واحده كما عم كل واحد من ذينك | الشكلين الاخرين والاول

12 شريطه واحده والشريطة التى تعم هذا الشكل والشكل الاول | انه لا ينبغى ان

13 تكون احدى مقدمتيه سالبه جزئيه وهذه الشريطه بعينها لزمت فى | الشكل الاول

14 من اشتراطنا فيه ان صغراه موجبه وكبراه كليه واما الشكلين الاخرين | فقد

15 تكون فى كل واحد منها مقدمه هى سالبه جزئيه واما الشريطه التى عمت | كل

واحد من ذينك الشكلين الاخرين والاول فنحن نذكرها وهى ان كبرى الشكل

16 الثانى ينبغى | ان تكون كليه كما اشترط فى كبرى الشكل الاول وصغرى

17 الشكل الثالث ينبغى ان تكون موجبه | كما اشترط فى صغرى الشكل الاول

18 فكما ان شريطه الشكل الاول التى عمت مقدمتيه وهو | ان ليس فيها سالبه

جزئيه كذلك عمت مقدمتى الشكل المزيد وكما ان الشريطه التى خصت

19 | كبراه وهو ان تكون كليه كذلك خصت كبرى الثانى وكما ان الشريطه التى

20 خصت صغراه | وهى ان تكون موجبه كذلك خصت صغرى الشكل الثالث

21 واما الشريطه التى خصت هذا | الشكل المزيد فهو ان لا تجمع فيه ازدواج

22 صغراه موجبه كليه وكبراه موجبه كليه | كما خص الشكل الثانى بشريطه تخصه

23 دون الثلثه الاشكال الباقيه وهو ان تختلف مقدمتاه | فى الكيف فاما الشكل الثالث

125b1 فلم يختص بشريطه وحده وذلك ما يقال فيه ان فيه شريطتان || احداهما ان

2 تكون صغراه موجبه والشرط الاخر انه لا بد فيه من مقدمه كليه ليس | تخاص

به ان هذه الشريطه الاخيره لم تختص بها بل هى داخله فيما يعم الاشكال الاربعه

3 | وهو انه لا قياس فيها من جزئيتين ومن هاهنا اعنى ان لهذا الشكل الثالث شريطه

4 واحده | كثرت ضروبه المنتجه وصارت سته بخلاف سائر الاشكال الباقيه فان

5 ضروبها اقل | من ذلك فاما لم كان فى الاول اربعه اضرب منتجه وفى الثانى

6 ايضا اربعه اضرب وفى | الثالث سته اضرب وفى الشكل المزيد خمسه اضرب

7 فهذا شىء نبينه الان بانه لزم عن هذه | الشرايط وذلك ان عدد الازدواجات فى

8 كل واحد من الاشكال على ما توجبه القسمه | سته عشر ازدواجا اعنى الازدواجات

9 التى مقدماتها محصوره باسوار فانا لو ادخلنا | المهملات فى الجمله لكانت سته

10 وثلثين ازدواجا ولكن لما كانت المهمله قوتها قوه الجزئيه | وذلك انها محتمله ان

81

11 تكون كليه ومحتمله ان تكون جزئيه الا ان كونها كليه مشكوك فيه وكونها | جزئيه

معلوم متيقن لان ما يصدق على الكل يصدق على الجزء اقنا الجزئيه مقام المهمله

12 | والذى تبين به ان القسمه تقتضى فى المحصورات سته عشر ازدواجا هو هذا.

13 | ان المقدمتين لا تخلوا من ان تكونا جميعا كليتين او جميعا جزئيتين او تكونا كليه

14 وجزويه | او جزئيه وكليه فهذه اربعه ازدواجات وكل واحد من هذه الازدواجات

15 لا يخلوا | من اربعه احوال وهو ان تكونا جميعا سالبتين او جميعا موجبتين او تكونا

16 موجبه وسالبه | او سالبه وموجبه فاذا ضوعفت هذه الاربعه الاحوال الاخر

17 بالاربعه الاحوال الاول | جاء من ذلك سته عشر ازدواجا منها اربعه كليات وهى

18 هذه (١) كليتين موجبتين | (ب) كليتين سالبتين (ج) كليه موجبه وكليه سالبه

19 (د) كليه سالبه وكليه موجبه. | واربع جزئيات اخر تصير مع الاول ثمان وهى

20 هذه. (ه) جزئيتين موجبتين (و) | جزئيتين سالبتين (ذ) جزئيه موجبه وجزويه

21 سالبه (ح) جزئيه سالبه وجزئيه موجبه. | واربع اخر من كليه صغرى وجزئيه

22 كبرا تصير مع المتقدمه اثنا عشر وهى هذه | (ط) كليه موجبه وجزئيه موجبه

23 (ى) كليه سالبه وجزئيه سالبه (يا) كليه موجبه | وجزئيه سالبه (بب) كليه

سالبه وجزئيه موجبه. واربع اقترانات اخر تتركب || من مقدمتين صغراهما جزئيه   126a1

2 وكبراهما كليه تصير مع جميع ما تقدم من الازدواجات | سته عشر ازدواجا وهى

3 هذه (بج) جزئيه موجبه وكليه موجبه (بد) جزئيه سالبه | وكليه سالبه (به) جزئيه

4 موجبه وكليه سالبه (بو) جزئيه سالبه وكليه موجبه فهذه | السته عشر ازدواجا

5 تعقم منها بالشرائط الثلث التى اشترطناها عامه فى الاشكال | الاربعه ثمان

6 ازدواجات وذلك ان الشرائط الثلث هى انه لا قياس من جزئيتين ولا من سالبتين |

ولا من صغرى سالبه وكبرى جزئيه فبالشريطه الاولى وهى انه لا قياس من

7 جزئيتين | تعقم اربع ازدواجات وهى الخامس والسادس والسابع والثامن وباشتراطنا

8 انه | لا قياس من سالبتين تعقم ثلث اقترانات وهى الثانى والعاشر والرابع عشر

9 وباشتراطنا | انه لا قياس من صغرى سالبه وكبرى جزئيه تعقم مما تبقى ازدواج

10 واحد وهو الثانى عشر | فصارت الازدواجات(٦) العقم فى كل واحد من الاشكال

11 على طريق العموم ثمانيه ازدواجات | كما ذكرنا وباشتراطنا فى الشكل الاول

12 شريطتين تخصانه يلغوا اربع ازدواجات اخر | وذلك ان باشتراطنا فيه ان صغراه

---

⁶ In the MS: الازدوات.

13 موجبه يلغوا مما بقى ازدواجان وهما الثـــالث والسادس عشر | وباشتراطنا فيه ان

14 كبراه كليه يلغوا من السته الازدواجات الباقيه ازدواجان | وهما التاسع والحادى

15 عشر فتبقى الازدواجات المنتجه فى الشكل الاول اربعه وهى | الاول والثالث

16 والثالث عشر والخـامس عشر. وكذلك ايضا باشتراطنا فى الشكل الثانى | شريطتان

17 تبقى فيه من الثمانى الاقترانات الباقيه اربعه اضرب منتجه وذلك ان | احدى

شريطتيه هى احدى شريطتى الاول وهى ان تكون كبراه كليه فيلغوا منه

18 الاقترانان | اللذان لغيا فى الشكل الاول بهذه الشريطه وهما التاسع والحادى عشر

19 واما الشريطه | الثانيه التى تخصه فهى ان تختلف مقدمتاه فى الكيف فيلغوا منه

20 من الست البواقى ازدواجان | اخران وهما الاول والثالث عشر وتبقى له اربع ازدواجات

21 منتجه وهى الثالث والرابع | والخـامس عشر والسادس عشر وكذلك تكون اقترانات

22 الشكل الثالث المنتجه من الثمان | الباقيه سته ازدواجات لان الشريطه التى تخصه

23 شريطه واحده وهى احدى | شريطتى الاول اعنى ان تكون صغراه موجبه فيلغوا

منه اقترانان وهما الثالث والسادس عشر [7] || وهما اللذان سقطا فى الشكل الاول

126b1

2 بهذه الشريطه وتبقى ضروبه المنتجه كما قلنا سته وهى | الاول والرابع والتاسع

3 والحادى عشر والثالث عشر والخـامس عشر وبالشريطتين | اللتين اشترطناها فى

4 الشكل المزيد يلغوا من الثمان الباقيه ثلث اقترانات وذلك | ان احدى الشريطتين

5 كانت انه لا ينبغى ان تكون احدى مقدمتيه سالبه جزئيه فيلغوا | بذلك اقترانين

6 وهما الحادى عشر والسادس عشر وهذان الازدواجان كانا لغيا | فى الاول لمجموع

7 شريطتيه لانه لغى بكل شريطه من شريطتى الاول واحد من هذين | وبالشريطه

الاخرى وهو انه لا قياس فيه عن صغرى جزئيه موجبه وكبرى كليه موجبه

8 | يلغوا هذا الضرب وحده وهو الثالث عشر فتبقى ضروبه المنتجه خمسه وهى

9 الاول والثالث | والرابع والتاسع والخـامس عشر. ولانا قد ذكرنا ان عدد جميع

10 الازدواجات فى كل | واحد من الاشكال الاربعه سته عشر ازدواجا تكون

11 جملتها فى جميعها اربعه وستون | ازدواجا منها خمسه واربعون عقما وتسعه عشر ضربا

12 منتجه. وقد بقى مما ضمناه قبيل | ان نبرهن على الخمسه الاضرب التى ذكرنا

13 انها منتجه فى الشكل المزيد ونبين صحه ذلك وكذلك | نبين ان الاحد عشر

14 ضربا الباقيه عقم وهذا حين ابتدى بذلك على توالى الازدواجات | **فالضرب**

⁷ In the MS one only reads: والسا.

15 **الاول** من كليتين موجبتين تنتج موجبه جزئيه. مثال ذلك كل ا ب | وكل ج ا

16 فاقول انه ينتج بعض ب ج برهان ذلك انا نغير الترتيب بان نجعل | الكبرى

صغرى والصغرى كبرى فتصير هكذا كل ج ا وكل ا ب تنتج كل ج ب

17 بالضرب | الاول من الشكل الاول ونعكس هذه النتيجه فيصير بعض ب ج

18 وهو مطلوبنا ومثاله | من المواد كل ناطق حيوان وكل انسان ناطق فينتج بعض

19 الحيوان انسان **الثانى** | من كليتين سالبتين وهو عقيم لانه ينتج الايجاب الكلى

20 والسلب الكلى معا وما كان كذلك | فهو عقيم لانه لا ينتج شيئا واحدا بل الشىء

21 وضده فليس بقياس لان القياس على ما حده | ارسطوطاليس قول مؤلف من

22 اقاويل يلزم عنها لذاتها شىء واحد من الاضطرار | وهذا فلا يلزم عنه شىء

23 واحد وبهذا الطريق بين ارسطوطاليس الاقترانات العقم | فى كتاب انالوطيقا

الاولى. مثال ذلك ما ينتج الايجاب الكلى لا حجر واحد انسان || ولا حيوان واحد 127a1

2 حجر فكل انسان حيوان ومثال ما ينتج السلب الكلى لا حجر واحد انسان | ولا

فرس واحد حجر فلا انسان واحد فرس. **الثالث** وهو الضرب الثانى من المنتجه

3 | من كليتين كبراهما موجبه وصغراهما سالبه تنتج سالبه كليه. مثاله لا شىء

4 من ا ب | وكل ج ا ينتج فلا شىء من ب ج وذلك انا نغير ترتيبه بان نجعل

5 الصغرى كبرى | والكبرى صغرى فيصير هكذا كل ج ا ولا شىء من ا ب

6 ينتج فلا شىء من ج ب بالضرب | الثانى من الشكل الاول ونعكس هذه

7 النتيجه فتصير ولا شىء من ب ج وهو الذى | اردنا. ومثاله من المواد لا حيوان

8 واحد حجر وكل انسان حيوان فينتج لا حجر واحد | انسان. **الرابع** وهو الضرب

9 الثالث من المنتجه. من كليتين كبراهما سالبه | وصغراهما موجبه تنتج سالبه جزئيه

10 مثاله كل ا ب ولا شىء من ج ا ينتج فليس كل | ب ج وذلك ان نعكس كلتى

11 المقدمتين فيصير هكذا بعض ب ا لان الموجبه الكليه | تنعكس جزئيه موجبه

12 ولا شىء من ا ج لان السالبه الكليه تنعكس مثل نفسها فينتج فليس | كل ب ج

بالضرب الرابع من الشكل الاول. ومثاله من المواد كل انسان حيوان ولا فرس

13 | واحد انسان فليس كل حيوان فرس. **الضرب الخامس** من جزئيتين موجبتين

14 | وهو عقيم لانه ينتج الايجاب الكلى والسلب الكلى على ما سنذكره عاما لهذه

15 الاقترانات | الاربعه التى من جزئيتين. **الضرب السادس** من جزئيتين سالبتين

16 وهو عقيم | ايضا ينتج المتضادتان. **الضرب السابع** من جزئيه موجبه صغرى

17 وجزئیه | سالبه کبری وهو عقیم ایضا ینتج المتضادتین معا **الضرب الثامن** من

18 جزئیه | سالبه صغری وجزئیه موجبه کبری وهو عقیم والحدود التی تنتج الایجاب

19 الکلی لهذه الاربعه الازدواجات هی الانسان والحیوان والجسم بان نجعل الحیوان

20 الحد | المشترك والانسان الحد الاصغر والجسم الاکبر واما الحدود التی تنتج السلب

21 22 الکلی | فهذه الابیض والانسان والطائر بان نجعل الابیض الحد المشترك والانسان | الحد

23 الاصغر والطائر الحد الاکبر . **الضرب التاسع** وهو الرابع من الضروب | المنتجه

من کلیه موجبه صغری وجزئیه موجبه کبری تنتج موجبه جزئیه مثال ذلك

|| کل ا ب وبعض ج ا فاقول انه ینتج بعض ب ج برهان ذلك انا نجعل کل 127b1

2 | واحده من المقدمتین فی موضع صاحبها فتصیر هکذا بعض ج ا وکل ا ب

3 | نتج فبعض ج ب بالضرب الثالث من الشکل الاول وبعکس هذه النتیجه

4 فتصیر | بعض ب ج وذلك ما اردنا ومثاله من المواد کل انسان حیوان وبعض

5 الناطق | انسان فبعض الحیوان ناطق. **الضرب العاشر** من کلیه سالبه صغری

6 وجزئیه | سالبه کبری. وهو عقیم ینتج المتضادتین معا. مثال ما ینتج الایجاب

7 الکلی لا انسان | واحد فرس ولیس کل نامی انسان فکل فرس نامی ومثال ما

8 ینتج السلب الکلی لا انسان | واحد حجر ولیس کل نامی انسان فلا حجر واحد

9 نامی. **الضرب الحادی عشر** | من کلیه موجبه صغری وجزئیه سالبه کبری وهو

10 عقیم ینتج المتضادتین مثال ما | ینتج الایجاب الکلی کل انسان حیوان ولیس

11 کل جسم انسان فکل حیوان جسم ومثال | ما ینتج السلب الکلی کل حیوان

12 حساس ولیس کل حجر حیوان فلا حساس واحد حجر | ولا ینبغی ان نسبق

13 الی الظن انا وهمنا فی هذا المثال الذی ینتج السلب الکلی بقولنا لیس | کل حجر

14 حیوان فان کان الواجب ان نقول لا حجر واحد حیوان وذلك ان قولنا | لیس کل

15 حجر حیوان صادق ایضا لان السالبه الجزئیه تصدق مع السالبه الکلیه وقد | اقتدینا

بارسطوطالیس فی هذا المثال وذلك انه فعل مثل ذلك فی مواضع من کتاب

16 | انالوطیقا الاولی منها الاقتران الذی من سالبه جزئیه صغری وموجبه کلیه کبری

17 | فی الشکل الاول حین اراد ان یبین انه غیر منتج قال بالفاظه نصا هکذا. مثال

18 | ذلك ان ا موجوده فی کل ب و ب غیر موجوده لبعض ج او غیر موجوده

19 لکل ج | فحدود ذلك الحی والانسان والابیض ثم المأخوذ من الابیض ما لا یقال

20 علیه الانسان | ولکن ذلك ققنس والثلج والحی مقول علی کل هذا وغیر مقول علی

85

21 شىء من ذلك. | كذلك ان يجعل الانسان هو الحد الاوسط فى كلى المثالين التى

22 تنتج الايجاب الكلى والسلب | (؟)[8] هو الحد الاكبر فى كلى المثالين واما الحد

23 الاصغر فجعله فيما ينتج الايجاب | (؟)[9] السلب الكلى الثلج فحى من هذا فى

128a1 الايجاب الكلى اقتران هكذا. ‖ ليس كل ققنس انسان وكل انسان حيوان فينتج

2 كل ققنس حيوان ومعلوم ان قوله ليس | كل ققنس انسان لا يعطى ان الققنس

3 انسان لان السالبه الجزئيه تصدق مع السالبه | الكليه وكذلك استعمله فى المثال

4 الاخر وهو الذى ينتج السلب الكلى ليس كـل ثلج انسان | وكل انسان حيوان

5 فلا ثلج واحد انسان. **الضرب الثانى عشر** من كليه سالبه صغرى | وجزئيـه موجبه

6 كبرى وهو عقيم لانه ينتج المتضادتين مثال ما ينتج الايجاب الكلى | لا شىء من

7 الناس فرس وبعض النامى انسان ينتج فكل فرس نامى ومثال ما ينتج السلب الكلى

8 | لا شىء من الناس حجر وبعض الحيوان انسان فلا شىء من الحجر حيوان وقد

9 زعم دنحا ان | هذا الضرب منتج مثال ما ذكره لا شىء ا ب وبعض ج ا فزعم انه

10 ينتج ليس كل | ب ج وذلك بان نغير الترتيب ونجعل كل واحده من المقدمتين

11 فى موضع الاخرى | فتقصير هكذا بعض ج ا ولا شىء من ا ب فينتج فليس

12 ج ب بالضرب الرابع من الشكل | الاول لكن عندنا ان هذا غير منتج لان

13 المطلوب ان ينتج ليس كل ب ج لان الحد الاكبر | هو ج وهو انتج عكس

14 هذا ليس كل ج ب وليس تنعكس هذه النتيجه لانها سالبه جزئيه | فهذا انتج

15 عكس المطلوب لا المطلوب فان كان بعد هذا الضرب منتجا فليجعل فى

16 | الشكل الاول ضربين اخرين منتجين وهما الضرب الذى صغره سالبه كليه

17 وكبراه كليه | موجبه والضرب الذى صغراه كليه سالبه وكبراه جزئيه موجبه مثال

18 ذلك لا شىء | من ب ا وكل ا ج او بعض ا ج ينتج ليس كل ج ب لانا ان

19 عكسنا كلتا المقدمتين صار | الضربان هكذا وهما بعض ج ا ولا شىء من ا ب

20 فينتج ليس كل ج ب بالضرب الرابع | من الشكل الاول ولكن المطلوب كان

21 بعض ب ج لا عكسه فهذا لم يجعل ارسطوطاليس | هذين الضربين منتجين وان

22 كان بعض القدما قد جعلها منتجين فالاعتراض عليه كما ذكرنا | فى فسخ

23 ذلك وانه ينتج عكس المطلوب ولا ينتج المطلوب **الضرب الثالث عشر** من

24 جزيه | موجبه صغرى وكليه موجبه كبرى وهو عقيم لانه ينتج الضدين معا مثال

---

[8] Illegible passage of 3–4 words.   [9] Illegible passage of 3–4 words.

22	ذلك فى الايجاب ‖ الكلى بعض الحيوان انسان وكل ناطق حيوان فكل انسان
23	ناطق ومثال السلب الكلى بعض ‖ الحيوان انسان وكل فرس حيوان فلا انسان واحد
128b1	فرس وهذا الضرب ايضا جعله ‖ دنحا منتجا لانه جعل كل واحده من المقدمتين
2	فى موضع الاخرى والزم عنهما ايجابا ‖ جزئيا ولم يعلم انه اذا جعل الصغرى فى
3	موضع الكبرى جاء من هذا ضرب فى الشكل الاول ‖ مركب من صغرى كليه
4	موجبه وكبرى موجبه وهو غير منتج لان من شريطه الاول ‖ ان تكون كبراه كليه
5	فهذا وهم منه فى معرفه الشكل الاول. **الضرب الرابع عشر** ‖ من جزئيه سالبه
6	صغرى وكليه سالبه كبرى وهو عقيم لانه نتج الضدين معا. مثال ذلك ‖ فى
	الايجاب الكلى ليس كل انسان صهال ولا فرس واحد انسان فكل صهال فرس
7	ومثاله ‖ فى السلب الكلى ليس كل حيوان انسان ولا حجر واحد حيوان فلا انسان
8	واحد حجر. ‖ **الضرب الخامس عشر** وهو الضرب الخامس من الضروب
9	المنتجه من جزئيه موجبه ‖ صغرى وكليه سالبه كبرى ينتج جزئيه سالبه مثاله بعض
10	ا ب ولا شىء من ج ا ينتج ‖ فليس كل ب ج وذلك انا نعكس كلتى المقدمتين
11	فيصير هكذا بعض ب ا ولا شىء من ا ج ‖ فينتج فليس كل ب ج بالضرب
12	الرابع من الشكل الاول مثاله من المواد بعض الحيوان ‖ ابيض ولا حجر واحد
13	حيوان فليس كل ابيض حجر. **الضرب السادس عشر** ‖ من جزئيه سالبه صغرى
14	وكليه موجبه كبرى وهو عقيم ينتج المتضادتين معا. مثال ذلك ‖ فيما ينتج الايجاب
	الكلى ليس كل حيوان انسان وكل ناطق حيوان فكل انسان حيوان وفيما
15	‖ ينتج السلب الكلى ليس كل حيوان انسان وكل فرس حيوان فلا انسان واحد
16	فرس. ‖ فهذه هى الضروب المنتجه والعقم قد تبينت الا ان ما بيناه منها انما اخذناه
17	فيها ‖ كلتا المقدمتين على انهما مطلقتين فاما اذا كانت المقدمتان جميعا ضروريتين
18	‖ او ممكنتين او مختلطه من هذه الثلثه الاصناف اعنى المطلق والضرورى والممكن
19	‖ فانه يحتاج الى بيان اخر ولان هذا الفن من العلم قد كان القدماء يفرزونه عن
20	‖ الاول ولهذا ما يعرفه الحدث من الاسكندرانيين بجزء لا يقرا فنحن مفردوه
21	‖ على حياله فى مقاله تتلوا هذه ان شاء الله تعالى.
	تمت المقاله والحمد لله وحده
22	

REFERENCES

Note.—Only works in certain limited categories are listed here. There is no attempt to give here a general listing of all the works we have had occasion to cite.

I. Galen's *Introduction to Logic*

1. MINOIDES MINAS [or Mynas] (ed.). *Galēnou eisagōgē dialektikē* (Paris, 1845).

2. CARL PRANTL. *Geschichte der Logik im Abendlande*, vol. I (München, 1855 ; photoreprint Berlin and Darmstatt, 1955) ; see especially pp. 570–574 and 591–610.

3. CAROLUS (KARL) KALBFLEISCH (ed.). *Galeni institutio logica* (Leipzig, Teubner, 1896).

4. EMILIO ORTH (tr.). *Galenos : Einführung in die Logik* (Rome, 1938).

5. JÜRGEN MAU (tr.). *Galen : Einführung in die Logik* (Berlin, Deutsche Akademie der Wissenschaften zu Berlin, 1960).

6. KARL KALBFLEISCH. " Ueber Galens Einleitung in die Logik," *Jahrbuch für klassische Philologie* ; Supplement 23 (1897), pp. 679–708.

7. JOHN S. KIEFFER (tr.). *Galen's Institutio Logica* (Baltimore, Johns Hopkins Press, 1964).

II. Studies of Galen's Logic

1. CHARLES DAREMBERG. *Fragments du Commentaire de Galien sur le Timée de Platon, suivis d'un Essai sur Galien considéré comme philosophe* (Paris and Leipzig, 1848). [The *Essai* contains a short section (pp. 8–10) on the " Influence de Galien sur la logique."]

2. CARL PRANTL. *Geschichte der Logik im Abendlande*, vol. I (München, 1855 ; photoreprint Berlin and Darmstatt, 1955) ; see especially pp. 570–574 and 591–610.

3. EMMANUEL CHAUVET. " La logique de Galien," *Séances et travaux de l'Académie des sciences morales et politiques*, N.S., vol. 17 (1882), pp. 430–451 ; reprinted in the author's book, *La philosophie des medicins grecs* (Paris, 1886).

4. IWAN VON MÜLLER. " Ueber Galens Werk vom Wissenschaftlichen Beweis," *Abhandlungen der Münchener Akademie der Wissenschaften*, Philosophisch-historische Klasse, vol. 20 (1895), pp. 403–478.

5. JAMES W. STAKELUM. *Galen and the Logic of Propositions* (Rome, 1940).

6. JAMES W. STAKELUM. " Why ' Galenian ' Figure ? " *The New Scholasticism*, vol. 16 (1942), pp. 289–296.

7. JAN LUKASIEWICZ. *Aristotle's Syllogistic* (Oxford, 1951 ; 2d ed., 1957). [See Chapter 2.]

REFERENCES

III. Tracts on the Fourth Syllogistic Figure

1. Ibn al-Ṣalāḥ (d. 1153). The treatise at issue in the present book.

2. Jacob Zabarella (d. 1589). *Liber quarta syllogismorum figura.* In his *Opera* (Leiden, 1587), pp. 41–53 ; his *Logica* (Padua, 1587) ; and his *Opera logica* (Basel, 1594), cols. 101–132. [I have used the Basel edition.]

3. Émile Thouverez. " La IVème figure du syllogisme," *Archiv für Geschichte der Philosophie* (= Erste Abteilung of the *Archiv für Philosophie*), vol. 15 (1902), pp. 4–110.

4. Paul Henle. " On the Fourth Figure of the Syllogism," *Philosophy of Science*, vol. 16 (1949), pp. 94–104.

5. Lynn E. Rose. " Aristotle's Syllogistic and the Fourth Figure," *Mind*, vol. 74 (1965), pp. 382–389.

INDEX

Abailard, Peter, 26, 31
al-Abharī, 10, 11
Afnan, S. M., 18
al-Akhḍarī, 11
Albalag, Isaac, 11
Albert the Great, 31, 32, 65
Aldrich, Henry, 23, 30, 31, 35, 36, 38
Alexander of Aphrodisias, 7, 8, 14, 17, 26, 29, 30, 53
Alexandrians, 74
Ammonius, 2
Anonymous Scholiast, 2–3, 21
Appuleius, 36, 65
Aquinas, 13
Aristotle, 1, 2, 4, 5, 7, 8, 9, 10, 12, 13, 14, 15, 16, 17, 19, 20, 22, 23, 24, 25, 26, 27, 28, 29, 30, 34, 35, 39, 43, 44, 45, 46, 47, 53, 54, 59
Arnauld, Antoine, 24, 34, 35
ibn al-ʿAssāl, 10
Avenzoar, 8
Averroes, 2, 3, 4, 6, 8, 9, 13, 20, 24, 33, 35, 44, 50
Avicenna, 7, 8, 9, 10, 11, 12, 13, 14, 18, 19, 24, 50

ibn Bājjah (Avempace), 7, 8, 9
al-Bajūrī, 11
ibn Bakhtīshūʿ, Jibrīl, 5
Bar Hebraeus, 11
Baumstark, Anton, 50
Benegno, Giorgio, 32
Bergsträsser, Gotthelf, 5, 6
Bochenski, I. M., 1, 11, 30, 31, 32, 46, 65
Boethius, 18, 30, 36
Boole, George, 38
Bosanquet, Bernard, 39
Bossuet, 40
Bowen, Francis, 38, 42
Bradley, F. H., 39
Brerewood, Edward, 36
Brockelmann, C., 49
Burana, J. F., 33
Burgersdicius, Franco, 36

Campbell, D., 8
Casiri, M., 9
Chauvet, Emmanuel, 88
Cheikho, L., 10, 17
Cohen, M. R., 45
Couturat, Louis, 40, 42, 48
Crackenthorpe, Richard, 34, 36
Crusius, Christian August, 36, 37

Daremberg, Charles, 88
Derenbourg, H., 8
Dietericus, Cunradus Theodoricus, 36
Dinḥā (Denḥā), 13, 50, 53, 71, 72
Dopp, Joseph, 40
Dunlop, D. M., 9
Duns Scotus, 31
Duval-Jouve, J., 35

Eck, Johann, 32
Eddé, Paul, 10, 17
Erdmann, Benno, 39
Eudemus, 2, 18, 29
Euler, L., 35

al-Fārābī, Abū Naṣr, 6, 7, 8, 9, 12, 13, 20, 26, 53, 54
Forget, J., 9, 18

Galen of Pergamon, 1–9, 10, 11, 12, 13, 14, 15, 17, 18, 19, 20, 21, 24, 26, 33, 35, 45, 49, 50, 53, 88
Gassendi, Pierre, 25, 34
Gerhard, C. I., 35
al-Ghazzālī, 11
Giles of Rome, 31
Goichon, A. M., 24
Grabmann, M., 23
Graf, Georg, 5
Gratry, A., 40
Gredt, Joseph, 40

Hallam, A., 25
Hamelin, O., 23
Hamilton, Sir William, 38
Hartshorne, C., 40
Hārūn al-Rashīd, 5
Hegel, 39
Henle, Paul, 43, 89
Herbart, J. F., 39
Hispanus, Petrus, 13
Horten, Max, 10
Houtsma, M. Th., 19
Howell, W. S., 36
Ḥunain ibn Isḥāq, 5, 6

ʿĪsō ibn Yaḥyā, 6
Isho bar Nūn, 50
Italus, Ioannes, 2

Janssens, H. F., 9, 11
Jevons, W. Stanley, 38, 41
Johnson, W. E., 38, 42

91